the
poetry
of
Elizabeth
Barrett
Browning

ISBN

9781788885171

the poetry of Elizabeth Barrett Browning

This edition published in 2019 by Arcturus Publishing Limited
26/27 Bickels Yard, 151–153 Bermondsey Street,
London SE1 3HA

AD006517UK

Printed in the UK

Contents

Introduction

Elizabeth Barrett Browning was born on 6 March 1806 in Durham, England. She had a happy childhood growing up in the English countryside of the Malvern Hills. When she was fifteen, it is thought Elizabeth suffered a spinal injury that permanently damaged her health. In 1832, the Barrett family moved to Sidmouth in Devon and then to London in 1836. Elizabeth published her first collection of poems, titled *The Seraphim and Other Poems*, in 1838. Tragedy struck the family later that same year, when Elizabeth's brother Edward drowned, causing her to develop a phobia of meeting new people. She continued writing poetry, however, releasing another successful collection called Poems in 1844.

Robert Browning began writing love poems to Elizabeth in January 1845, and their romance (which they diligently hid from her father) began in the summer. The couple married secretly on 12 September 1846, but Elizabeth later described her fear of marrying Browning in *Sonnets from the Portuguese* (1850). In 1856, Elizabeth's father Edward died, still carrying a grudge against his daughter for her elopement. Meanwhile, the pair moved to Pisa together, where Elizabeth wrote *The Runaway Slave at Pilgrim's Point* (1848-1849). She gave birth to their only son in Florence in 1849.

Elizabeth completed her hugely successful *Aurora Leigh* (1857), now considered an early feminist piece, during a trip to London. Late in her life, she became intensely interested in religion, the occult, and Italian politics to an almost acute degree. Sadly, she never fully recovered from her initial illness and injury, and in 1861, she died from a severe chill.

Stanzas on the Death of Lord Byron

He was, and is not! Graecia's trembling shore,
Sighing through all her palmy groves, shall tell
That Harold's pilgrimage at last is o'er –
Mute the impassioned tongue, and tuneful shell,
That erst was wont in noblest strains to swell –
Hush'd the proud shouts that rode Aegaea's wave!
For lo! the great Deliv'rer breathes farewell!
Gives to the world his mem'ry and a grave –
Expiring in the land he only lived to save!

Mourn, Hellas, mourn! and o'er thy widow'd brow,
For aye, the cypress wreath of sorrow twine;
And in thy new-form'd beauty, desolate, throw
The fresh-cull'd flowers on his sepulchral shrine.
Yes! let that heart whose fervour was all thine,
In consecrated urn lamented be!
That generous heart where genius thrill'd divine,
Hath spent its last most glorious throb for thee –
Then sank amid the storm that made thy children free!

Britannia's Poet! Graecia's hero, sleeps!
And Freedom, bending o'er the breathless clay,
Lifts up her voice, and in her anguish weeps!
For us, a night hath clouded o'er our day,
And hush'd the lips that breath'd our fairest lay.
Alas! and must the British lyre resound
A requiem, while the spirit wings away
Of him who on its strings such music found,
And taught its startling chords to give so sweet a sound!

The theme grows sadder – but my soul shall find
A language in those tears! No more – no more!
Soon, 'midst the shriekings of the tossing wind,
The 'dark blue depths' he sang of, shall have bore
Our all of Byron to his native shore!
His grave is thick with voices – to the ear
Murm'ring an awful tale of greatness o'er;
But Memory strives with Death, and lingering near,
Shall consecrate the dust of Harold's lonely bier!

The Autumn

Go, sit upon the lofty hill,
And turn your eyes around,
Where waving woods and waters wild
Do hymn an autumn sound.
The summer sun is faint on them —
The summer flowers depart —
Sit still — as all transform'd to stone,
Except your musing heart.

How there you sat in summer-time,
May yet be in your mind;
And how you heard the green woods sing
Beneath the freshening wind.
Though the same wind now blows around,
You would its blast recall;
For every breath that stirs the trees,
Doth cause a leaf to fall.

Oh! like that wind, is all the mirth
That flesh and dust impart:
We cannot bear its visitings,
When change is on the heart.
Gay words and jests may make us smile,
When Sorrow is asleep;
But other things must make us smile,
When Sorrow bids us weep!

The dearest hands that clasp our hands, —
Their presence may be o'er;
The dearest voice that meets our ear,

That tone may come no more!
Youth fades; and then, the joys of youth,
Which once refresh'd our mind,
Shall come – as, on those sighing woods,
The chilling autumn wind.

Hear not the wind – view not the woods;
Look out o'er vale and hill-
In spring, the sky encircled them –
The sky is round them still.
Come autumn's scathe – come winter's cold –
Come change – and human fate!
Whatever prospect Heaven doth bound,
Can ne'er be desolate.

The Soul's Travelling

I dwell amid the city ever.
The great humanity which beats
Its life along the stony streets,
Like a strong and unsunned river
In a self-made course,
I sit and hearken while it rolls.
Very sad and very hoarse,
Certes, is the flow of souls:
Infinitest tendencies
By the finite prest and pent,
In the finite, turbulent,
How we tremble in surprise,
When sometimes, with an awful sound,
God's great plummet strikes the ground!

The champ of the steeds on the silver bit,
As they whirl the rich man's carriage by;
The beggar's whine as he looks at it, –
But it goes too fast for charity;
The trail on the street of the poor man's broom,
That the lady who walks to her palace-home,
On her silken skirt may catch no dust;
The tread of the business-men who must
Count their per-cents by the paces they take;
The cry of the babe unheard of its mother
Though it lie on her breast, while she thinks of her other
Laid yesterday where it will not wake;
The flower-girl's prayer to buy roses and pinks,
Held out in the smoke, like stars by day;
The gin-door's oath that hollowly chinks

Guilt upon grief and wrong upon hate;
The cabman's cry to get out of the way
The dustman's call down the area-grate,
The young maid's jest, and the old wife's scold,
The haggling talk of the boys at a stall,
The fight in the street which is backed for gold,
The plea of the lawyers in Westminster Hall;
The drop on the stones of the blind man's staff
As he trades in his own grief's sacredness;
The brothel shriek, and the Newgate laugh,
The hum upon 'Change, and the organ's grinding –
The grinder's face being nevertheless
Dry and vacant of even woe,
While the children's hearts are leaping so
At the merry music's winding;
The black-plumed funeral's creeping train,
Long and slow (and yet they will go
As fast as Life, though it hurry and strain!),
Creeping the populous houses through,
And nodding their plumes at either side, –
At many a house where an infant, new
To the sunshiny world, has just struggled and cried, –
At many a house, where sitteth a bride
Trying tomorrow's coronals
With a scarlet blush today:
  Slowly creep the funerals,
As none should hear the noise and say,
'The living, the living must go away
    To multiply the dead.'
  Hark! an upward shout is sent!
In grave strong joy from tower to steeple
    The bells ring out –

The trumpets sound, the people shout,
The young queen goes to her Parliament.
She turneth round her large blue eyes,
More bright with childish memories
Than royal hopes, upon the people:
On either side she bows her head
  Lowly, with a queenly grace,
And smile most trusting-innocent,
As if she smiled upon her mother;
The thousands press before each other
  To bless her to her face;
And booms the deep majestic voice
Through trump and drum, – 'May the queen rejoice
    In the people's liberties!' –

I dwell amid the city,
And hear the flow of souls in act and speech,
For pomp or trade, for merrymake or folly;
I hear the confluence and sum of each,
  And that is melancholy! –
Thy voice is a complaint, O crownèd city,
The blue sky covering thee like God's great pity.

  O blue sky! it mindeth me
  Of places where I used to see
  Its vast unbroken circle thrown
  From the far pale-peakèd hill
  Out to the last verge of ocean,
  As by God's arm it were done
  Then for the first time, with the emotion
  Of that first impulse on it still.
  Oh, we spirits fly at will,

Faster than the wingèd steed
Whereof in old book we read,
With the sunlight foaming back
From his flanks to a misty wrack,
And his nostril reddening proud
As he breasteth the steep thundercloud, –
Smoother than Sabrina's chair
Gliding up from wave to air,
While she smileth debonair
Yet holy, coldly and yet brightly,
Like her own mooned waters nightly,
Through her dripping hair.

Very fast and smooth we fly,
Spirits, though the flesh be by.
All looks feed not from the eye,
Nor all hearings from the ear;
We can hearken and espy
Without either; we can journey
Bold and gay as knight to tourney,
And though we wear no visor down
To dark our countenance, the foe
Shall never chafe us as we go.

I am gone from peopled town!
It passeth its street-thunder round
My body which yet hears no sound:
For now another sound, another
Vision, my soul's senses have –
O'er a hundred valleys deep,
Where the hills' green shadows sleep
Scarce known (because the valley-trees

Cross those upland images),
O'er a hundred hills, each other
Watching to the western wave,
I have travelled, – I have found
The silent, lone, remembered ground.

I have found a grassy niche
Hollowed in a seaside hill,
As if the ocean-grandeur which
Is aspectable from the place
Had struck the hill as with a mace
Sudden and cleaving. You might fill
That little nook with the little cloud
Which sometimes lieth by the moon
To beautify a night of June.
A cavelike nook, which, opening all
To the wide sea, is disallowed
From its own earth's sweet pastoral;
Cavelike, but roofless overhead,
And made of verdant banks instead
Of any rocks, with flowerets spread,
Instead of spar and stalactite,
Cowslips and daisies, gold and white:
Such pretty flowers on such green sward,
You think the sea they look toward
Doth serve them for another sky
As warm and blue as that on high.

And in this hollow is a seat,
And when you shall have crept to it,
Slipping down the banks too steep
To be o'erbrowsèd by the sheep,

Do not think – though at your feet
The cliff's disrupt – you shall behold
The line where earth and ocean meet.
You sit too much above to view
The solemn confluence of the two:
You can hear them as they greet;
You can hear that evermore
Distance-softened noise, more old
Than Nereid's singing, – the tide spent
Joining soft issues with the shore
In harmony of discontent, –
And when you hearken to the grave
Lamenting of the underwave,
You must believe in earth's communion,
Albeit you witness not the union.

Except that sound, the place is full
Of silences, which when you cull
By any word, it thrills you so
That presently you let them grow
To meditation's fullest length
Across your soul with a soul's strength:
And as they touch your soul, they borrow
Both of its grandeur and its sorrow,
That deathly odour which the clay
Leaves on its deathlessness alway.

Alway! alway? must this be?
Rapid Soul from city gone,
Dost thou carry inwardly
What doth make the city's moan?
Must this deep sigh of thine own

Haunt thee with humanity?
Green visioned banks that are too steep
To be o'erbrowsèd by the sheep,
May all sad thoughts adown you creep
Without a shepherd? – Mighty sea,
Can we dwarf thy magnitude,
And fit it to our straitest mood? –
O fair, fair Nature! are we thus
Impotent and querulous
Among thy workings glorious,
Wealth and sanctities, – that still
Leave us vacant and defiled,
And wailing like a soft-kissed child,
Kissed soft against his will?

God, God!
With a child's voice I cry,
Weak, sad, confidingly –
God, God!
Thou knowest, eyelids, raised not always up
Unto Thy love, (as none of ours are), droop
    As ours, o'er many a tear!
Thou knowest, though Thy universe is broad,
Two little tears suffice to cover all:
Thou knowest, Thou, who art so prodigal
Of beauty, we are oft but stricken deer
Expiring in the woods – that care for none
Of those delightsome flowers they die upon.

O blissful Mouth which breathed the mournful breath
We name our souls, self-spoilt! – by that strong passion
Which paled Thee once with sighs, – by that strong death

Which made Thee once unbreathing – from the wrack
Themselves have called around them, call them back,
Back to Thee in continuous aspiration!
    For here, O Lord,
For here they travel vainly, – vainly pass
From city-pavement to untrodden sward,
Where the lark finds her deep nest in the grass
Cold with the earth's last dew. Yea, very vain
The greatest speed of all these souls of men,
Unless they travel upward to the throne,
Where sittest THOU the satisfying ONE,
With help for sins and holy perfectings
For all requirements – while the archangel, raising
Unto Thy face his full ecstatic gazing,
Forgets the rush and rapture of his wings.

Consolation

All are not taken; there are left behind
Living Belovèds, tender looks to bring
And make the daylight still a happy thing,
And tender voices, to make soft the wind:
But if it were not so — if I could find
No love in all this world for comforting,
Nor any path but hollowly did ring
Where 'dust to dust' the love from life disjoin'd;
And if, before those sepulchres unmoving
I stood alone (as some forsaken lamb
Goes bleating up the moors in weary dearth)
Crying 'Where are ye, O my loved and loving?' —
I know a voice would sound, 'Daughter, I AM.
Can I suffice for Heaven and not for earth?'

The Sleep

OF all the thoughts of God that are
Borne inward into souls afar,
Along the Psalmist's music deep,
Now tell me if that any is
For gift or grace surpassing this –
'He giveth His beloved, sleep'?

What would we give to our beloved?
The hero's heart to be unmoved,
The poet's star-tun'd harp to sweep,
The patriot's voice to teach and rouse,
The monarch's crown to light the brows? –
He giveth His beloved, sleep.

What do we give to our beloved?
A little faith all undisproved,
A little dust to overweep,
And bitter memories to make
The whole earth blasted for our sake:
He giveth His beloved, sleep.

'Sleep soft, beloved!' we sometimes say
Who have no tune to charm away
Sad dreams that through the eyelids creep:
But never doleful dream again
Shall break the happy slumber when
He giveth His beloved, sleep.

O earth, so full of dreary noises!
O men, with wailing in your voices!

O delved gold, the wailers heap!
O strife, O curse, that o'er it fall!
God strikes a silence through you all,
And giveth His beloved, sleep.

His dews drop mutely on the hill,
His cloud above it saileth still,
Though on its slope men sow and reap:
More softly than the dew is shed,
Or cloud is floated overhead,
He giveth His beloved, sleep.

Ay, men may wonder while they scan
A living, thinking, feeling man
Confirm'd in such a rest to keep;
But angels say, and through the word
I think their happy smile is *heard* —
'He giveth His beloved, sleep.'

For me, my heart that erst did go
Most like a tired child at a show,
That sees through tears the mummers leap,
Would now its wearied vision close,
Would childlike on His love repose
Who giveth His beloved, sleep.

And friends, dear friends, when it shall be
That this low breath is gone from me,
And round my bier ye come to weep,
Let One, most loving of you all,
Say, 'Not a tear must o'er her fall!
He giveth His beloved, sleep.'

A Romance of the Ganges

SEVEN maidens 'neath the midnight
  Stand near the river-sea,
Whose water sweepeth white around
  The shadow of the tree.
The moon and earth are face to face,
  And earth is slumbering deep;
The wave-voice seems the voice of dreams
  That wander through her sleep.
                  The river floweth on.

What bring they 'neath the midnight,
  Beside the river-sea?
They bring the human heart wherein
  No nightly calm can be, –
That droppeth never with the wind,
  Nor drieth with the dew:
O, calm it God! Thy calm is broad
  To cover spirits, too.
                  The river floweth on.

The maidens lean them over
  The waters, side by side,
And shun each other's deepening eyes,
  And gaze adown the tide:
For each within a little boat
  A little lamp hath put,
And heaped for freight some lily's weight
  Or scarlet rose half shut.
                  The river floweth on.

Of shell of cocoa carven,
 Each little boat is made:
Each carries a lamp, and carries a flower,
 And carries a hope unsaid.
And when the boat hath carried the lamp
 Unquenched, till out of sight,
The maidens are sure that love will endure, –
 But love will fail with light.
                              The river floweth on.

Why, all the stars are ready
 To symbolise the soul,
The stars untroubled by the wind,
 Unwearied as they roll;
And yet the soul by instinct sad
 Reverts to symbols low, –
To that small flame whose very name,
 Breathed o'er it, shakes it so!
                              The river floweth on.

Six boats are on the river,
 Seven maidens on the shore,
While still above them steadfastly
 The stars shine evermore.
Go, little boats, go soft and safe,
 And guard the symbol spark!
The boats aright go safe and bright
 Across the waters dark.
                              The river floweth on.

The maiden Luti watcheth
  Where onwardly they float.
That look in her dilating eyes
  Might seem to drive her boat;
Her eyes still mark the constant fire,
  And kindling unawares
That hopeful while she lets a smile
  Creep silent through her prayers.
                   The river floweth on.

The smile, – where hath it wandered?
  She riseth from her knee,
She holds her dark, wet locks away, –
  There is no light to see!
She cries a quick and bitter cry,
  'Nuleeni, launch me thine!
We must have light abroad to-night,
  For all the wreck of mine.'
                   The river floweth on.

'I do remember watching
  Beside this river-bed,
When on my childish knee was laid
  My dying father's head.
I turned mine own, to keep the tears
  From falling on his face, –
What doth it prove when death and love
  Choose out the self-same place?'
                   The river floweth on.

'They say the dead are joyful
  The death-change here receiving.

Who say, – ah me! who dare to say
    Where joy comes to the living?
Thy boat, Nuleeni! look not sad, –
    Light up the waters rather!
I weep no faithless lover where
    I wept a loving father.'
                           The river floweth on.

'My heart foretold his falsehood
    Ere my little boat grew dim:
And though I closed mine eyes to dream
    That one last dream of him,
They shall not now be wet to see
    The shining vision go:
From earth's cold love I look above
    To the holy house of snow.'
                           The river floweth on.

'Come thou, – thou never knewest
    A grief, that thou shouldst fear one!
Thou wearest still the happy look
    That shines beneath a dear one!
Thy humming-bird is in the sun,
    Thy cuckoo in the grove,
And all the three broad worlds, for thee
    Are full of wandering love.'
                           The river floweth on.

'Why, maiden, dost thou loiter?
    What secret wouldst thou cover?
That peepul cannot hide thy boat,
    And I can guess thy lover:

I heard thee sob his name in sleep, –
    It was a name I knew, –
Come, little maid, be not afraid,
    But let us prove him true!'
                    The river floweth on.

The little maiden cometh,
    She cometh shy and slow;
I ween she seeth through her lids,
    They drop adown so low:
Her tresses meet her small bare feet, –
    She stands and speaketh nought,
Yet blusheth red as if she said
    The name she only thought.
                    The river floweth on.

She knelt beside the water,
    She lighted up the flame,
And o'er her youthful forehead's calm
    The fitful radiance came:
'Go, little boat, go soft and safe,
    And guard the symbol spark!'
Soft, safe doth float the little boat
    Across the waters dark.
                    The river floweth on.

Glad tears her eyes have blinded;
    The light they cannot reach:
She turneth with that sudden smile
    She learnt before her speech, –
'I do not hear his voice! the tears
    Have dimmed my light away!

But the symbol light will last to-night,
    The love will last for aye.'
                        The river floweth on.

Then Luti spake behind her, –
    Outspake she bitterly:
'By the symbol light that lasts to-night,
    Wilt vow a vow to me?'
Nuleeni gazeth up her face, –
    Soft answer maketh she:
'By loves that last when lights are past,
    I vow that vow to thee!'
                        The river floweth on.

An earthly look had Luti
    Though her voice was deep as prayer, –
'The rice is gathered from the plains
    To cast upon thine hair;
But when he comes, his marriage-band
    Around thy neck to throw,
Thy bride-smile raise to meet his gaze,
    And whisper, – There is one betrays,
While Luti suffers woe.'
                        The river floweth on.

'And when in seasons after,
    Thy little bright-faced son
Shall lean against thy knee and ask
    What deeds his sire hath done,
Press deeper down thy mother-smile
    His glossy curls among,
View deep his pretty childish eyes, –

And whisper, – There is none denies,
When Luti speaks of wrong.'

                The river floweth on.

Nuleeni looked in wonder,
  Yet softly answered she –
'By loves that last when lights are past,
  I vowed that vow to thee.
But why glads it thee that a bride-day be
  By a word of woe defiled?
That a word of wrong take the cradle-song
  From the ear of a sinless child?'
'Why?' Luti said, and her laugh was dread,
  And her eyes dilated wild —
'That the fair new love may her bridegroom prove,
  And the father shame the child!'

                The river floweth on.

'Thou flowest still, O river,
  Thou flowest 'neath the moon, –
Thy lily hath not changed a leaf,
  Thy charméd lute a tune!
He mixed his voice with thine, – and his
  Was all I heard around;
But now, beside his chosen bride,
  I hear the river's sound.'

                The river floweth on.

'I gaze upon her beauty
  Through the tresses that enwreathe it:
The light above thy wave is hers, –
  My rest, alone beneath it.

O, give me back the dying look
  My father gave thy water!
Give back! and let a little love
  O'erwatch his weary daughter!'
                    The river floweth on.

'Give back!' she hath departed, –
  The word is wandering with her,
And the stricken maidens hear afar
  The step and cry together.
Frail symbols? None are frail enow
  For mortal joys to borrow!
While bright doth float Nuleeni's boat,
  She weepeth, dark with sorrow.
                    The river floweth on.

Isobel's Child

So find we profit,
By losing of our prayers.
                            Shakespeare

ℒₑ

I

To rest the weary nurse has gone,
  An eight-day watch had watchèd she,
Still rocking beneath sun and moon
  The baby on her knee,
Till Isobel its mother said, ·
'The fever waneth – wend to bed,
  For now the watch comes round to me.'

II

Then wearily the nurse did throw
Her pallet in the darkest place
  Of that sick room, and slept and dreamed:
  For, as the gusty wind did blow
  The night-lamp's flare across her face,
She saw or seemed to see, but dreamed,
  That the poplars tall on the opposite hill,
  The seven tall poplars on the hill,
  Did clasp the setting sun until
  His rays dropped from him, pined and still
    As blossoms in frost!
Till he waned and paled, so weirdly crossed,
To the colour of moonlight which doth pass

Over the dank ridged churchyard grass.
    The poplars held the sun, and he
The eyes of the nurse that they should not see,
Not for a moment, the babe on her knee,
Though she shuddered to feel that it grew to be
    Too chill, and lay too heavily.

III

She only dreamed; for all the while
'T was Lady Isobel that kept
The little baby, – and it slept
Fast, warm, as if its mother's smile,
Laden with love's dewy weight,
And red as rose of Harpocrate
Dropt upon its eyelids, pressed
Lashes to cheek in a sealèd rest.

IV

And more and more smiled Isobel
To see the baby sleep so well –
    She knew not that she smiled.
Against the lattice, dull and wild
Drive the heavy droning drops,
Drop by drop, the sound being one –
As momently time's segments fall
On the ear of God, who hears through all
    Eternity's unbroken monotone.
And more and more smiled Isobel
To see the baby sleep so well –
    She knew not that she smiled.
The wind in intermission stops
Down in the beechen forest,

Then cries aloud
  As one at the sorest,
  Self-stung, self-driven,
And rises up to its very tops,
Stiffening erect the branches bowed,
Dilating with a tempest-soul
The trees that with their dark hands break
Through their own outline and heavy roll
Shadows as massive as clouds in heaven,
Across the castle lake.
And more and more smiled Isobel
To see the baby sleep so well;
She knew not that she smiled;
She knew not that the storm was wild.
Through the uproar drear she could not hear
The castle clock which struck anear –
She heard the low, light breathing of her child.

V

  O sight for wondering look!
While the external nature broke
Into such abandonment,
While the very mist, heart-rent
By the lightning, seemed to eddy
Against nature, with a din,
A sense of silence and of steady
Natural calm appeared to come
From things without, and enter in
  The human creature's room.

VI

   So motionless she sat,
The babe asleep upon her knees,
You might have dreamed their souls had gone
Away to things inanimate,
In such to live, in such to moan;
And that their bodies had ta'en back,
In mystic change, all silences
That cross the sky in cloudy rack,
Or dwell beneath the reedy ground
In waters safe from their own sound.
   Only she wore
The deepening smile I named before,
And that a deepening love expressed;
And who at once can love and rest?

VII

In sooth the smile that then was keeping
Watch upon the baby sleeping,
Floated with its tender light
Downward, from the drooping eyes,
Upward, from the lips apart,
Over cheeks which had grown white
   With an eight-day weeping.
All smiles come in such a wise,
Where tears shall fall or have of old –
Like northern lights that fill the heart
   Of heaven in sign of cold.

VIII

   Motionless she sat..
Her hair had fallen by its weight

On each side of her smile, and lay
Very blackly on the arm
Where the baby nestled warm,
Pale as baby carved in stone
Seen by glimpses of the moon
  Up a dark cathedral aisle.
But, through the storm, no moonbeam fell
Upon the child of Isobel –
Perhaps you saw it by the ray
  Alone of her still smile.

IX

A solemn thing it is to me
To look upon a babe that sleeps;
Wearing in its spirit-deeps
The undeveloped mystery
Of our Adam's taint and woe,
Which, when they developed be,
Will not let it slumber so!
Lying new in life beneath
The shadow of the coming death,
With that soft, low, quiet breath,
  As if it felt the sun!
Knowing all things by their blooms,
Not their roots, yea, sun and sky,
Only by the warmth that comes
Out of each, – earth, only by
The pleasant hues that o'er it run, –
And human love, by drops of sweet
White nourishment still hanging round
The little mouth so slumber-bound.
All which broken sentiency

And conclusion incomplete,
Will gather and unite and climb
To an immortality
Good or evil, each sublime,
Through life and death to life again.
O little lids, now folded fast,
Must ye learn to drop at last
Our large and burning tears?
O warm quick body, must thou lie,
When the time comes round to die,
Still, from all the whirl of years,
Bare of all the joy and pain? –
O small frail being, wilt thou stand
  At God's right hand,
Lifting up those sleeping eyes
Dilated by great destinies,
To an endless waking? thrones and seraphim,
Through the long ranks of their solemnities,
Sunning thee with calm looks of Heaven's surprise,
  But thine alone on Him? –
Or else, self-willed, to tread the Godless place,
(God keep thy will!), feel thine own energies
Cold, strong, objectless, like a dead man's clasp,
The sleepless deathless life within thee, grasp, –
While myriad faces, like one changeless face,
With woe *not love's*, shall glass thee everywhere
And overcome thee with thine own despair?

X

More soft, less solemn images
Drifted o'er the lady's heart,
  Silently as snow.

She had seen eight days depart
Hour by hour, on bended knees,
With pale-wrung hands and prayings low
And broken, through which came the sound
Of tears that fell against the ground,
Making sad stops: – 'Dear Lord, dear Lord!'
She still had prayed, (the heavenly word,
Broken by an earthly sigh),
– 'Thou, who didst not erst deny
The mother-joy to Mary mild,
Blessèd in the blessèd child,
Which hearkened in meek babyhood
Her cradle-hymn, albeit used
To all that music interfused
In breasts of angels high and good!
Oh, take not, Lord, my babe away –
Oh, take not to thy songful heaven
The pretty baby thou hast given,
Or ere that I have seen him play
Around his father's knees and known
That he knew how my love has gone
   From all the world to him.
Think, God among the cherubim,
How I shall shiver every day
In Thy June sunshine, knowing where
The grave-grass keeps it from his fair
Still cheeks! and feel at every tread
His little body which is dead
And hidden in thy turfy fold,
Doth make thy whole warm earth a-cold!
O God, I am so young, so young –
I am not used to tears at nights

Instead of slumber – not to prayer
With sobbing lips and hands out-wrung!
Thou knowest all my prayings were
'I bless Thee, God, for past delights –
Thank God!' I am not used to bear
Hard thoughts of death; the earth doth cover
No face from me of friend or lover.
And must the first who teaches me
The form of shrouds and funerals, be
Mine own first-born belovèd? he
Who taught me first this mother-love?
Dear Lord who spreadest out above
Thy loving, transpiercèd hands to meet
All lifted hearts with blessing sweet, –
Pierce not my heart, my tender heart,
Thou madest tender! Thou who art
So happy in Thy heaven alway!
Take not mine only bliss away!'

XI
She so had prayed: and God, who hears
Through seraph-songs the sound of tears,
From that belovèd babe had ta'en
The fever and the beating pain.
And more and more smiled Isobel
To see the baby sleep so well
(She knew not that she smiled, I wis),
Until the pleasant gradual thought
Which near her heart the smile enwrought,
Now soft and slow, itself, did seem
To float along a happy dream,
    Beyond it into speech like this.

XII

'I prayed for thee, my little child,
And God has heard my prayer!
And when thy babyhood is gone,
We two together, undefiled
By men's repinings, will kneel down
Upon His earth which will be fair
(Not covering thee, sweet!) to us twain,
And give Him thankful praise.'

XIII

Dully and wildly drives the rain:
Against the lattices drives the rain.

XIV

'I thank Him now, that I can think
   Of those same future days,
Nor from the harmless image shrink
   Of what I there might see —
Strange babies on their mothers' knee,
Whose innocent soft faces might
From off mine eyelids strike the light,
   With looks not meant for me!'

XV

Gustily blows the wind through the rain,
As against the lattices drives the rain.

XVI

'But now, O baby mine, together
We turn this hope of ours again
To many an hour of summer weather,

When we shall sit and intertwine
Our spirits, and instruct each other
In the pure loves of child and mother!
Two human loves make one divine.'

XVII

The thunder tears through the wind and
   the rain,
As full on the lattices drives the rain.

XVIII

'My little child, what wilt thou choose?
Now let me look at thee and ponder.
What gladness, from the gladnesses
Futurity is spreading under
Thy gladsome sight? Beneath the trees
Wilt thou lean all day, and lose
Thy spirit with the river seen
Intermittently between
The winding beechen alleys, –
Half in labour, half repose,
Like a shepherd keeping sheep,
Thou, with only thoughts to keep
Which never a bound will overpass,
And which are innocent as those
That feed among Arcadian valleys
   Upon the dewy grass?'

XIX

The large white owl that with age is blind,
That hath sat for years in the old tree hollow,
Is carried away in a gust of wind!

His wings could bear him not as fast
As he goeth now the lattice past –
He is borne by the winds; the rains do
  follow:
His white wings to the blast outflowing,
  He hooteth in going,
And still, in the lightnings, coldly glitter
  His round unblinking eyes.

XX

'Or, baby, wilt thou think it fitter
To be eloquent and wise, –
One upon whose lips the air
Turns to solemn verities,
For men to breathe anew, and win
A deeper-seated life within?
Wilt be a philosopher,
By whose voice the earth and skies
Shall speak to the unborn?
Or a poet, broadly spreading
The golden immortalities
Of thy soul on natures lorn
And poor of such, them all to guard
From their decay, – beneath thy treading,
Earth's flowers recovering hues of Eden, –
And stars, drawn downward by thy looks,
To shine ascendant in thy books?'

XXI

  The tame hawk in the castle-yard,
How it screams to the lightning, with its wet
Jagged plumes overhanging the parapet!

And at the lady's door the hound
  Scratches with a crying sound.

XXII

'But, O my babe, thy lids are laid
  Close, fast upon thy cheek, –
And not a dream of power and sheen
Can make a passage up between;
Thy heart is of thy mother's made,
  Thy looks are very meek;
And it will be their chosen place
To rest on some belovèd face,
As these on thine – and let the noise
Of the whole world go on, nor drown
  The tender silence of thy joys!
Or when that silence shall have grown
Too tender for itself, the same
Yearning for sound, – to look above
And utter its one meaning, LOVE,
  That He may hear His name!'

XXIII

No wind, no rain, no thunder!
The waters had trickled not slowly,
The thunder was not spent,
Nor the wind near finishing.
Who would have said that the storm was diminishing?
No wind, no rain, no thunder!
Their noises dropped asunder
From the earth and the firmament,
From the towers and the lattices,
Abrupt and echoless

As ripe fruits on the ground unshaken wholly –
   As life in death!
And sudden and solemn the silence fell,
Startling the heart of Isobel
   As the tempest could not.
Against the door went panting the breath
Of the lady's hound whose cry was still,
And she, constrained howe'er she would not,
Lifted her eyes, and saw the moon
Looking out of heaven alone
  Upon the poplared hill, –
  A calm of God, made visible
  That men might bless it at their will.

XXIV
The moonshine on the baby's face
Falleth clear and cold.
The mother's looks have fallen back
To the same place;
Because no moon with silver rack,
Nor broad sunrise in jasper skies,
   Has power to hold
   Our loving eyes,
Which still revert, as ever must
Wonder and Hope, to gaze on the dust.

XXV
The moonshine on the baby's face
  Cold and clear remaineth:
The mother's looks do shrink away, –
The mother's looks return to stay,
  As charmèd by what paineth.
Is any glamour in the case?

Is it dream or is it sight?
Hath the change upon the wild
Elements, that sign the night,
   Passed upon the child?
It is not dream, but sight! –

XXVI

The babe has awakened from sleep,
And unto the gaze of its mother
Bent over it, lifted another!
Not the baby-looks that go
Unaimingly to and fro,
But an earnest gazing deep,
Such as soul gives soul at length,
When, by work and wail of years,
It winneth a solemn strength,
   And mourneth as it wears.
A strong man could not brook
With pulse unhurried by fears
To meet that baby's look
O'erglazed by manhood's tears –
The tears of a man full grown,
With a power to wring our own,
In the eyes all undefiled
Of a little three-months' child!
To see that babe-brow wrought
By the witnessing of thought,
To judgement's prodigy!
And the small soft mouth unweaned,
By mother's kiss o'erleaned,
(Putting the sound of loving
Where no sound else was moving,

Except the speechless cry),
   Quickened to mind's expression,
   Shaped to articulation,
Yea, uttering words – yea, naming woe,
In tones that with it strangely went,
Because so baby-innocent,
As the child spake out to the mother, so: –

XXVII

'O mother, mother, loose thy prayer!
   Christ's name hath made it strong.
It bindeth me, it holdeth me
With its most loving cruelty,
From floating my new soul along
   The happy heavenly air.
It bindeth me, it holdeth me
In all this dark, upon this dull
Low earth, by only weepers trod! –
It bindeth me, it holdeth me! –
Mine angel looketh sorrowful
   Upon the face of God.

XXVIII

'Mother, mother, can I dream
Beneath your earthly trees?
I had a vision and a gleam –
I heard a sound more sweet than these
   When rippled by the wind:
Did you see the Dove with wings
Bathed in golden glisterings
From a sunless light behind,
Dropping on me from the sky

Soft as mother's kiss, until
I seemed to leap and yet was still?
Saw you how His love-large eye
Looked upon me mystic calms,
Till the power of His divine
Vision was indrawn to mine?

XXIX

'Oh, the dream within the dream!
I saw celestial places even.
Oh, the vistas of high palms,
Making finites of delight
Through the heavenly infinite –
Lifting up their green still tops
   To the heaven of Heaven!
Oh, the sweet life-tree that drops
Shade like light across the river
Glorified in its for-ever
   Flowing from the Throne!
Oh, the shining holinesses
Of the thousand, thousand faces
God-sunned by the throned ONE!
And made intense with such a love,
That though I saw them turned above,
Each loving seemed for also me!
And, oh, the Unspeakable, the HE,
The manifest in secrecies,
Yet of mine own heart partaker, –
With the overcoming look
Of One who hath been once forsook,
   And blesseth the forsaker.
Mother, mother, let me go

Toward the Face that looketh so.
Through the mystic wingèd Four
Whose are inward, outward eyes
Dark with light of mysteries,
And the restless evermore
'Holy, holy, holy,' – through
The sevenfold Lamps that burn in view
Of cherubim and seraphim, –
Through the four-and-twenty crowned
Stately elders white around,
Suffer me to go to Him!

XXX

'Is your wisdom very wise,
Mother, on the narrow earth,
Very happy, very worth
That I should stay to learn?
Are these air-corrupting sighs
Fashioned by unlearnèd breath?
Do the students' lamps that burn
All night, illumine death?
Mother, albeit this be so,
Loose thy prayer and let me go
Where that bright chief angel stands
Apart from all his brother bands,
Too glad for smiling, having bent
In angelic wilderment
O'er the depths of God, and brought
Reeling thence, one only thought
To fill his own eternity.
He the teacher is for me! –
He can teach what I would know –
Mother, mother, let me go!

XXXI

'Can your poet make an Eden
    No winter will undo,
And light a starry fire while heeding
    His hearth's is burning too?
Drown in music the earth's din,
And keep his own wild soul within
The law of his own harmony? –
Mother, albeit this be so,
Let me to my Heaven go!
A little harp me waits thereby –
A harp whose strings are golden all,
And tuned to music spherical,
Hanging on the green life-tree
Where no willows ever be.
Shall I miss that harp of mine?
Mother, no! – the Eye divine
Turned upon it, makes it shine;
And when I touch it, poems sweet
Like separate souls shall fly from it,
Each to the immortal fytte.
We shall all be poets there,
Gazing on the chiefest Fair.

XXXII

'Love! earth's love! and can we love
Fixedly where all things move?
Can the sinning love each other?
    Mother, mother,
I tremble in thy close embrace,
I feel thy tears adown my face,
Thy prayers do keep me out of bliss –

O dreary earthly love!
Loose thy prayer and let me go
To the place which loving is
Yet not sad; and when is given
Escape to *thee* from this below,
Thou shalt behold me that I wait
For thee beside the happy Gate,
And silence shall be up in heaven
    To hear our greeting kiss.'

XXXIII

The nurse awakes in the morning sun,
And starts to see beside her bed
The lady with a grandeur spread
Like pathos o'er her face, – as one
God-satisfied and earth-undone.
    The babe upon her arm was dead!
And the nurse could utter forth no cry, –
She was awed by the calm in the mother's eye.

XXXIV

'Wake, nurse!' the lady said;
We are waking – he and I –
I, on earth, and he, in sky!
And thou must help me to o'erlay
With garment white, this little clay
Which needs no more our lullaby.

XXXV

'I changed the cruel prayer I made,
And bowed my meekened face, and prayed
That God would do His will! and thus

He did it, nurse! He parted us!
And His sun shows victorious
The dead calm face, – and I am calm,
And Heaven is hearkening a new psalm.

XXXVI

'This earthly noise is too anear,
Too loud, and will not let me hear
The little harp. My death will soon
Make silence.'

                     And a sense of tune,
A satisfied love meanwhile
Which nothing earthly could despoil,
Sang on within her soul.

XXXVII

                   Oh you,
Earth's tender and impassioned few,
Take courage to entrust your love
To Him so named, who guards above
  Its ends and shall fulfil!
Breaking the narrow prayers that may
Befit your narrow hearts, away
  In His broad, loving will.

Man and Nature

A sad man on a summer day
Did look upon the earth and say —

'Purple cloud the hill-top binding;
Folded hills the valleys wind in;
Valleys with fresh streams among you;
Streams with bosky trees along you;
Trees with many birds and blossoms;
Birds with music-trembling bosoms;
Blossoms dropping dews that wreathe you
To your fellow flowers beneath you;
Flowers that constellate on earth;
Earth that shakest to the mirth
Of the merry Titan Ocean,
All his shining hair in motion!
Why am I thus the only one
Who can be dark beneath the sun?'

But when the summer day was past,
He looked to heaven and smiled at last,
Self-answered so —
'Because, O cloud,
Pressing with thy crumpled shroud
Heavily on mountain top, —
Hills that almost seem to drop
Stricken with a misty death
To the valleys underneath, —
Valleys sighing with the torrent, —
Waters streaked with branches horrent, —
Branchless trees that shake your head

Wildly o'er your blossoms spread
Where the common flowers are found, –
Flowers with foreheads to the ground, –
Ground that shriekest while the sea
With his iron smiteth thee –
I am, besides, the only one
Who can be bright without the sun.'

Memory and Hope

Back-looking Memory
And prophet Hope both sprang from out the ground;
One, where the flashing of cherubic sword
Fell sad in Eden's ward,
And one, from Eden earth within the sound
Of the four rivers lapsing pleasantly,
What time the promise after curse was said,
'Thy seed shall bruise his head.'

Poor Memory's brain is wild,
As moonstruck by that flaming atmosphere
When she was born; her deep eyes shine and shone
With light that conquereth sun
And stars to wanner paleness year by year:
With odorous gums she mixeth things defiled,
She trampleth down earth's grasses green and sweet
With her far-wandering feet.

She plucketh many flowers,
Their beauty on her bosom's coldness killing;
She teacheth every melancholy sound
To winds and waters round;
She droppeth tears with seed where man is tilling
The rugged soil in his exhausted hours;
She smileth – ah me! in her smile doth go
A mood of deeper woe.

Hope tripped on out of sight,
Crowned with an Eden wreath she saw not wither,
And went a-nodding through the wilderness

With brow that shone no less
Than a sea-gull's wing, brought nearer by rough weather,
Searching the treeless rock for fruits of light;
Her fair quick feet being armed from stones and cold
   By slippers of pure gold.

   Memory did Hope much wrong
And, while she dreamed, her slippers stole away;
But still she wended on with mirth unheeding,
   Although her feet were bleeding,
Till Memory tracked her on a certain day,
And with most evil eyes did search her long
And cruelly, whereat she sank to ground
   In a stark deadly swound.

   And so my Hope were slain,
Had it not been that Thou wast standing near —
Oh Thou who saidest 'Live', to creatures lying
   In their own blood and dying!
For Thou her forehead to thine heart didst rear
And make its silent pulses sing again,
Pouring a new light o'er her darkened eyne
   With tender tears from thine.

   Therefore my Hope arose
From out her swound and gazed upon thy face,
And, meeting there that soft subduing look
   Which Peter's spirit shook,
Sank downward in a rapture to embrace
Thy pierced hands and feet with kisses close,
And prayed Thee to assist her evermore
   To 'reach the things before'.

The Weakest Thing

Which is the weakest thing of all
Mine heart can ponder?
The sun, a little cloud can pall
With darkness yonder?
The cloud, a little wind can move
Where'er it listeth?
The wind, a little leaf above,
Though sere, resisteth?

What time that yellow leaf was green,
My days were gladder;
But now, whatever Spring may mean,
I must grow sadder.
Ah me! a leaf with sighs can wring
My lips asunder –
Then is mine heart the weakest thing
Itself can ponder.

Yet, Heart, when sun and cloud are pined
And drop together,
And at a blast, which is not wind,
The forests wither,
Thou, from the darkening deathly curse
To glory breakest, –
The Strongest of the universe
Guarding the weakest!

Cowper's Grave

It is a place where poets crowned
　　May feel the heart's decaying –
It is a place where happy saints
　　May weep amid their praying:
Yet let the grief and humbleness,
　　As low as silence, languish –
Earth surely now may give her calm
　　To whom she gave her anguish.

O poets! from a maniac's tongue
　　Was poured the deathless singing!
O Christians! at your cross of hope
　　A hopeless hand was clinging!
O men! this man, in brotherhood,
　　Your weary paths beguiling,
Groaned inly while he taught you peace,
　　And died while ye were smiling!

And now, what time ye all may read
　　Through dimming tears his story –
How discord on the music fell
　　And darkness on the glory –
And how, when one by one, sweet sounds
　　And wandering lights departed,
He wore no less a loving face
　　Because so broken-hearted,

He shall be strong to sanctify
  The poet's high vocation,
And bow the meekest Christian down
  In meeker adoration;
Nor ever shall he be, in praise,
  By wise or good forsaken –
Named softly, as the household name
  Of one whom God hath taken.

With sadness that is calm not gloom
  I learn to think upon him;
With meekness that is gratefulness
  On God whose heaven hath won him –
Who suffered once the madness-cloud
  To His own love to blind him;
But gently led the blind along
  Where breath and bird could find him;
And wrought within his shattered brain
  Such quick poetic senses
As hills have language for, and stars
  Harmonious influences!
The pulse of dew upon the grass
  His own did calmly number;
And silent shadows from the trees
  Fell o'er him like a slumber.

The very world, by God's constraint,
  From falsehood's ways removing,
Its women and its men became,
  Beside him, true and loving! –
And timid hares were drawn from woods
  To share his home-caresses,

Uplooking to his human eyes
   With sylvan tendernesses.
But while, in blindness he remained
   Unconscious of that guiding,
And things provided came without
   The sweet sense of providing,
He testified this solemn truth,
   Though frenzy desolated —
Nor man nor nature satisfy,
   When only God created!

Like a sick child that knoweth not
   His mother while she blesses,
And droppeth on his burning brow
   The coolness of her kisses;
That turns his fevered eyes around —
   'My mother! where's my mother?' —
As if such tender words and looks
   Could come from any other! —

The fever gone, with leaps of heart
   He sees her bending o'er him;
Her face all pale from watchful love,
   Th' unweary love she bore him!
Thus woke the poet from the dream
   His life's long fever gave him,
Beneath those deep pathetic eyes
   Which closed in death to save him!

Thus? O, not thus! no type of earth
   Could image that awaking,
Wherein he scarcely heard the chant

Of seraphs, round him breaking –
Or felt the new immortal throb
   Of soul from body parted;
But felt those eyes alone, and knew,
   'My Saviour! not deserted!'

Deserted! Who hath dreamt that when
   The cross in darkness rested,
Upon the victim's hidden face
   No love was manifested?
What frantic hands outstretched have e'er
   Th' atoning drops averted –
What tears have washed them from the soul –
   That one should be deserted?

Deserted! God could separate
From His own essence rather;
And Adam's sins have swept between
The righteous Son and Father –
Yea! once, Immanuel's orphaned cry
His universe hath shaken –
It went up single, echoless,
'My God, I am forsaken!'

It went up from the Holy lips
Amid His lost creation,
That of the lost no son should use
Those words of desolation;
That earth's worst frenzies, marring hope,
Should mar not hope's fruition;
And I, on Cowper's grave, should see
His rapture, in a vision!

The Cry of the Children

'Pheu pheu, ti prosderkesthe m ommasin, tekna'
[Alas, alas, why do you gaze at me with your eyes,
my children.]

Medea

Do ye hear the children weeping, O my brothers,
　　Ere the sorrow comes with years?
They are leaning their young heads against their mothers,
　　And that cannot stop their tears.
The young lambs are bleating in the meadows,
　The young birds are chirping in the nest,
The young fawns are playing with the shadows,
　The young flowers are blowing toward the west –
But the young, young children, O my brothers,
　　They are weeping bitterly!
They are weeping in the playtime of the others,
　　In the country of the free.

Do you question the young children in the sorrow,
　　Why their tears are falling so?
The old man may weep for his tomorrow
　　Which is lost in Long Ago;
The old tree is leafless in the forest,
　The old year is ending in the frost,
The old wound, if stricken, is the sorest,
　The old hope is hardest to be lost.
But the young, young children, O my brothers,

Do you ask them why they stand
Weeping sore before the bosoms of their mothers,
    In our happy Fatherland?

They look up with their pale and sunken faces,
    And their looks are sad to see,
For the man's hoary anguish, draws and presses
    Down the cheeks of infancy;
'Your old earth,' they say, 'is very dreary;
    Our young feet,' they say, 'are very weak!'
Few paces have we taken, yet are weary –
    Our grave-rest is very far to seek.
Ask the aged why they weep, and not the children;
    For the outside earth is cold;
And we young ones stand without, in our
    bewildering,
    And the graves are for the old.'

'True,' say the children, 'it may happen
    That we die before our time:
Little Alice died last year – her grave is shapen
    Like a snowball, in the rime.
We looked into the pit prepared to take her:
    Was no room for any work in the close clay!
From the sleep wherein she lieth none will wake her,
    Crying, 'Get up, little Alice! it is day.'
If you listen by that grave, in sun and shower,
    With your ear down, little Alice never cries;
Could we see her face, be sure we should not know her,
    For the smile has time for growing in her eyes:
And merry go her moments, lulled and stilled in
    The shroud, by the kirk-chime!

It is good when it happens,' say the children,
    'That we die before our time.'

Alas, alas, the children! they are seeking
    Death in life, as best to have;
They are binding up their hearts away from breaking,
    With a cerement from the grave.
Go out, children, from the mine and from the city,
    Sing out, children, as the little thrushes do;
Pluck your handfuls of the meadow cowslips pretty,
    Laugh aloud, to feel your fingers let them through!
But they answer, 'Are your cowslips of the meadows
    Like our weeds anear the mine?
Leave us quiet in the dark of the coal-shadows,
    From your pleasures fair and fine!

'For oh,' say the children, 'we are weary,
    And we cannot run or leap;
If we cared for any meadows, it were merely
    To drop down in them and sleep.
Our knees tremble sorely in the stooping,
    We fall upon our faces, trying to go;
And, underneath our heavy eyelids drooping,
    The reddest flower would look as pale as snow;
For, all day, we drag our burden tiring
    Through the coal-dark, underground –
Or, all day, we drive the wheels of iron
    In the factories, round and round.

'For all day, the wheels are droning, turning, –
    Their wind comes in our faces, –
Till our hearts turn, – our heads, with pulses burning,

And the walls turn in their places:
Turns the sky in the high window blank and reeling,
  Turns the long light that drops down the wall,
Turn the black flies that crawl along the ceiling:
  All are turning, all the day, and we with all.
And all day, the iron wheels are droning,
    And sometimes we could pray,
'O ye wheels,' (breaking out in a mad moaning),
    'Stop! be silent for to-day!'

Aye be silent! Let them hear each other breathing
    For a moment, mouth to mouth!
Let them touch each other's hands, in a fresh wreathing
    Of their tender human youth!
Let them feel that this cold metallic motion
  Is not all the life God fashions or reveals:
Let them prove their living souls against the notion
  That they live in you, or under you, O wheels! –
Still, all day, the iron wheels go onward,
    Grinding life down from its mark;
And the children's souls, which God is calling sunward,
    Spin on blindly in the dark.

Now tell the poor young children, O my brothers,
    To look up to Him and pray –
So the blessèd One who blesseth all the others,
    Will bless them another day.
They answer, 'Who is God that He should hear us,
  While the rushing of the iron wheels is stirred?
When we sob aloud, the human creatures near us
  Pass by, hearing not, or answer not a word.
And we hear not (for the wheels in their resounding)

Strangers speaking at the door:
Is it likely God, with angels singing round Him,
    Hears our weeping any more?

'Two words, indeed, of praying we remember;
    And at midnight's hour of harm,
'Our Father,' looking upward in the chamber,
    We say softly for a charm.
We know no other words, except 'Our Father,'
  And we think that, in some pause of angels' song,
God may pluck them with the silence sweet to gather,
  And hold both within His right hand which is strong.
'Our Father!' If He heard us, He would surely
    (For they call Him good and mild)
Answer, smiling down the steep world very purely,
    'Come and rest with Me, My child.'

'But, no!' say the children, weeping faster,
    'He is speechless as a stone:
And they tell us, of His image is the master
    Who commands us to work on.
Go to!' say the children,—'up in Heaven,
  Dark, wheel-like, turning clouds are all we find.
Do not mock us; grief has made us unbelieving –
  We look up for God, but tears have made us blind.'
Do ye hear the children weeping and disproving,
    O my brothers, what ye preach?
For God's possible is taught by His world's loving,
    And the children doubt of each.

And well may the children weep before you!
    They are weary ere they run;

They have never seen the sunshine, nor the glory
    Which is brighter than the sun.
They know the grief of man, without its wisdom;
   They sink in man's despair, without its calm;
Are slaves, without the liberty in Christdom,
    Are martyrs, by the pang without the palm, –
Are worn, as if with age, yet unretrievingly
    The harvest of its memories cannot reap,—
Are orphans of the earthly love and heavenly.
    Let them weep! let them weep!

They look up, with their pale and sunken faces,
    And their look is dread to see,
For they mind you of their angels in high places,
    With eyes turned on Deity! –
'How long,' they say, 'how long, O cruel nation,
   Will you stand, to move the world, on a child's heart, –
Stifle down with a mailed heel its palpitation,
   And tread onward to your throne amid the mart?
Our blood splashes upward, O gold-heaper,
    And your purple shows your path;
But the child's sob in the silence curses deeper
    Than the strong man in his wrath.'

Grief

I tell you, hopeless grief is passionless;
That only men incredulous of despair,
Half-taught in anguish, through the midnight air
Beat upward to God's throne in loud access
Of shrieking and reproach. Full desertness,
In souls, as countries, lieth silent-bare
Under the blanching, vertical eye-glare
Of the absolute Heavens. Deep-hearted man, express
Grief for thy Dead in silence like to death: —
Most like a monumental statue set
In everlasting watch and moveless woe,
Till itself crumble to the dust beneath.
Touch it: the marble eyelids are not wet;
If it could weep, it could arise and go.

Lady Geraldine's Courtship

A Romance of the Age

Dear my friend and fellow student, I would lean my spirit
o'er you!
Down the purple of this chamber, tears should scarcely
run at will.
I am humbled who was humble. Friend,
I bow my head before you:
You should lead me to my peasants, – but their faces are
too still.

There's a lady – an earl's daughter, – she is proud and she
is noble,
And she treads the crimson carpet, and she breathes the
perfumed air,
And a kingly blood sends glances up, her princely eye to
trouble,
And the shadow of a monarch's crown is softened in her
hair.

She has halls among the woodlands, she has castles by the
breakers,
She has farms and she has manors, she can threaten and
command:
And the palpitating engines snort in steam across her
acres,
As they mark upon the blasted heaven the measure of the
land.

There are none of England's daughters who can show a
prouder presence;

Upon princely suitors' praying, she has looked in her
disdain.
She was sprung of English nobles, I was born of English
peasants;
What was I that I should love her, — save for competence
to pain?

I was only a poor poet, made for singing at her
casement,
As the finches or the thrushes, while she thought of other
things.
Oh, she walked so high above me, she appeared to my
abasement,
In her lovely silken murmur, like an angel clad in wings!

Many vassals bow before her as her carriage sweeps their
doorways;
She has blest their little children, — as a priest or queen
were she.
Far too tender, or too cruel far, her smile upon the poor
was,
For I thought it was the same smile which she used to
smile on me.

She has voters in the Commons, she has lovers in the
palace;
And of all the fair court-ladies, few have jewels half as
fine;
Oft the prince has named her beauty 'twixt the red wine
and the chalice.
Oh, and what was I to love her? my beloved, my
Geraldine!

Yet I could not choose but love her. I was born to poet-
uses,
To love all things set above me, all of good and all of fair:
Nymphs of mountain, not of valley, we are wont to call
the Muses
And in nympholeptic climbing, poets pass from mount to
star.

And because I was a poet, and because the public praised
me,
With a critical deduction for the modern writer's fault,
I could sit at rich men's tables, – though the courtesies
that raised me,
Still suggested clear between us the pale spectrum of the
salt.

And they praised me in her presence; –
'Will your book appear this summer?'
Then returning to each other – 'Yes, our plans are for the
moors.'
Then with whisper dropped behind me –
'There he is! the latest comer!
Oh, she only likes his verses! what is over, she endures.

'Quite low-born! self-educated! somewhat gifted though
by nature, –
And we make a point of asking him, – of being very
kind.
You may speak, he does not hear you! and besides, he
writes no satire, –
All these serpents kept by charmers leave the natural sting
behind.'

I grew scornfuller, grew colder, as I stood up there among
   them,
Till as frost intense will burn you, the cold scorning
   scorched my brow;
When a sudden silver speaking, gravely cadenced, over-
   rung them,
And a sudden silken stirring touched my inner nature
   through.

I looked upward and beheld her. With a calm and regnant
   spirit,
Slowly round she swept her eyelids, and said clear before
   them all –
'Have you such superfluous honour, sir, that able to confer it
You will come down, Mister Bertram, as my guest to
   Wycombe Hall?'

Here she paused, – she had been paler at the first word of
   her speaking,
But, because a silence followed it, blushed somewhat, as
   for shame,
Then, as scorning her own feeling, resumed calmly – 'I
   am seeking
More distinction than these gentlemen think worthy of
   my claim.

'Ne'ertheless, you see, I seek it – not because I am a
   woman'
(Here her smile sprang like a fountain and, so, overflowed
   her mouth),
'But because my woods in Sussex have some purple
   shades at gloaming

Which are worthy of a king in state, or poet in his
  youth.

'I invite you, Mister Bertram, to no scene for worldly
  speeches —
Sir, I scarce should dare — but only where
God asked the thrushes first —
And if you will sing beside them, in the covert of my
  beeches,
I will thank you for the woodlands, ... for the human
  world, at worst.'

Then she smiled around right childly, then she gazed
  around right queenly,
And I bowed — I could not answer; alternated light and
  gloom —
While as one who quells the lions, with a steady eye
  serenely,
She, with level fronting eyelids, passed out stately from
  the room.

Oh, the blessèd woods of Sussex, I can hear them still
  around me,
With their leafy tide of greenery still rippling up the
  wind.
Oh, the cursèd woods of Sussex! where the hunter's
  arrow found me,
When a fair face and a tender voice had made me mad
  and blind!

In that ancient hall of Wycombe, thronged the numerous
  guests invited,

And the lovely London ladies trod the floors with gliding
feet;
And their voices low with fashion, not with feeling, softly
freighted
All the air about the windows, with elastic laughters sweet.

For at eve, the open windows flung their light out on the
terrace,
Which the floating orbs of curtains did with gradual
shadow sweep,
While the swans upon the river, fed at morning by the
heiress,
Trembled downward through their snowy wings at music
in their sleep.

And there evermore was music, both of instrument and
singing,
Till the finches of the shrubberies grew restless in the
dark;
But the cedars stood up motionless, each in a moonlight
ringing,
And the deer, half in the glimmer, strewed the hollows of
the park.

And though sometimes she would bind me with her
silver-corded speeches
To commix my words and laughter with the converse and
the jest,
Oft I sat apart, and gazing on the river through the
beeches,
Heard, as pure the swans swam down it, her pure voice
o'erfloat the rest.

In the morning, horn of huntsman, hoof of steed, and
  laugh of rider,
Spread out cheery from the court-yard till we lost them
  in the hills,
While herself and other ladies, and her suitors left beside
  her,
Went a-wandering up the gardens through the laurels and
  abeles.

Thus, her foot upon the new-mown grass, bareheaded,
  with the flowing
Of the virginal white vesture gathered closely to her
  throat, –
And the golden ringlets in her neck just quickened by her
  going,
And appearing to breathe sun for air, and doubting if to
  float, –

With a bunch of dewy maple, which her right hand held
  above her,
And which trembled a green shadow in betwixt her and
  the skies,
As she turned her face in going, thus, she drew me on to
  love her,
And to worship the divineness of the smile hid in her
  eyes.

For her eyes alone smile constantly: her lips have serious
  sweetness,
And her front is calm – the dimple rarely ripples on the
  cheek;

But her deep blue eyes smile constantly, as if they in
  discreetness
Kept the secret of a happy dream she did not care to
  speak.

Thus she drew me the first morning, out across into the
  garden,
And I walked among her noble friends and could not
  keep behind.
Spake she unto all and unto me – 'Behold, I am the
  warden
Of the song-birds in these lindens, which are cages to
  their mind.

'But within this swarded circle, into which the lime-walk
  brings us,
Whence the beeches, rounded greenly, stand away in
  reverent fear,
I will let no music enter, saving what the fountain sings
  us,
Which the lilies round the basin may seem pure enough
  to hear.

'The live air that waves the lilies waves the slender jet of
  water
Like a holy thought sent feebly up from soul of fasting
  saint:
Whereby lies a marble Silence, sleeping! (Lough the
  sculptor wrought her)
So asleep she is forgetting to say Hush! – a fancy
  quaint.

'Mark how heavy white her eyelids! not a dream between
   them lingers,
And the left hand's index droppeth from the lips upon
   the cheek;
While the right hand, – with the symbol rose held slack
   within the fingers, –
Has fallen backward in the basin – yet this Silence will
   not speak!

'That the essential meaning growing may exceed the
   special symbol,
Is the thought as I conceive it: it applies more high and
   low.
Our true noblemen will often through right nobleness
   grow humble,
And assert an inward honour by denying outward show.'

'Nay, your Silence,' said I, 'truly, holds her symbol rose
   but slackly, –
Yet she holds it, – or would scarcely be a Silence to our
   ken;
And your nobles wear their ermine on the outside, or
   walk blackly
In the presence of the social law as mere ignoble men.

'Let the poets dream such dreaming! madam, in these
   British islands
'Tis the substance that wanes ever, 'tis the symbol that
   exceeds.
Soon we shall have nought but symbol! and, for statues
   like this Silence,
Shall accept the rose's image – in another case, the weed's.'

'Not so quickly,' she retorted, – 'I confess, where'er you
  go, you
Find for things, names – shows for actions, and pure gold
  for honour clear;
But when all is run to symbol in the Social, I will throw
  you
The world's book which now reads dryly, and sit down
  with Silence here.'

Half in playfulness she spoke, I thought, and half in
  indignation;
Friends who listened, laughed her words off, while her
  lovers deemed her fair:
A fair woman, flushed with feeling, in her noble-lighted
  station
Near the statue's white reposing – and both bathed in
  sunny air! –

With the trees round, not so distant but you heard their
  vernal murmur,
And beheld in light and shadow the leaves in and
  outward move,
And the little fountain leaping toward the sun-heart to be
  warmer,
Then recoiling in a tremble from the too much light
  above.

'Tis a picture for remembrance. And thus, morning after
  morning,
Did I follow as she drew me by the spirit to her feet.
Why, her greyhound followed also! dogs – we both were
  dogs for scorning –

To be sent back when she pleased it and her path lay
  through the wheat.

And thus, morning after morning, spite of vows and spite
  of sorrow,
Did I follow at her drawing, while the week-days passed
  along, –
Just to feed the swans this noontide, or to see the fawns
  tomorrow,
Or to teach the hill-side echo some sweet Tuscan in a
  song.

Aye, for sometimes on the hill-side, while we sat down in
  the gowans,
With the forest green behind us, and its shadow cast
  before,
And the river running under, and across it from the
  rowans
A brown partridge whirring near us, till we felt the air it
  bore, –

There, obedient to her praying, did I read aloud the
  poems
Made to Tuscan flutes, or instruments more various of our
  own;
Read the pastoral parts of Spenser – or the subtle inter-
  flowings
Found in Petrarch's sonnets – here's the book – the leaf is
  folded down!

Or at times a modern volume, – Wordsworth's solemn-
  thoughted idyl,

Howitt's ballad-verse, or Tennyson's enchanted reverie, –
Or from Browning some 'Pomegranate', which, if cut
   deep down the middle,
Shows a heart within blood-tinctured, of a veined
   humanity.

Or at times I read there, hoarsely, some new poem of my
   making:
Poets ever fail in reading their own verses to their
   worth, –
For the echo in you breaks upon the words which you
   are speaking,
And the chariot-wheels jar in the gate through which you
   drive them forth.

After, when we were grown tired of books, the silence
   round us flinging
A slow arm of sweet compression, felt with beatings at
   the breast,
She would break out, on a sudden, in a gush of woodland
   singing,
Like a child's emotion in a god – a naiad tired of
   rest.

Oh, to see or hear her singing! scarce I know which is
   divinest –
For her looks sing too – she modulates her gestures on
   the tune;
And her mouth stirs with the song, like song; and when
   the notes are finest,
'Tis the eyes that shoot out vocal light and seem to swell
   them on.

Then we talked – oh, how we talked! her voice, so
   cadenced in the talking,
Made another singing – of the soul! a music without
   bars;
While the leafy sounds of woodlands, humming round
   where we were walking,
Brought interposition worthy-sweet, – as skies about the
   stars.

And she spake such good thoughts natural, as if she
   always thought them;
She had sympathies so rapid, open, free as bird on
   branch,
Just as ready to fly east as west, whichever way besought
   them,
In the birchen-wood a chirrup, or a cock-crow in the
   grange.

In her utmost lightness there is truth – and often she
   speaks lightly,
Has a grace in being gay which even mournful souls
   approve,
For the root of some grave earnest thought is understruck
   so rightly
As to justify the foliage and the waving flowers above.

And she talked on – we talked, rather! upon all things,
   substance, shadow,
Of the sheep that browsed the grasses, of the reapers in
   the corn,
Of the little children from the schools, seen winding
   through the meadow –

Of the poor rich world beyond them, still kept poorer by
  its scorn.

So, of men, and so, of letters – books are men of higher
  stature,
And the only men that speak aloud for future times to hear;
So, of mankind in the abstract, which grows slowly into
  nature,
Yet will lift the cry of 'progress', as it trod from sphere to
  sphere.

And her custom was to praise me when I said, – 'The Age
  culls simples,
With a broad clown's back turned broadly to the glory of
  the stars.
We are gods by our own reck'ning, and may well shut up
  the temples,
And wield on, amid the incense-steam, the thunder of
  our cars.

'For we throw out acclamations of self-thanking,
  self-admiring,
With, at every mile run faster, — "O the wondrous
  wondrous age!"
Little thinking if we work our souls as nobly as our iron,
Or if angels will commend us at the goal of pilgrimage.

'Why, what is this patient entrance into nature's deep
  resources,
But the child's most gradual learning to walk upright
  without bane?

When we drive out, from the cloud of steam, majestical
  white horses,
Are we greater than the first men who led black ones by
  the mane?

'If we trod the deeps of ocean, if we struck the stars in
  rising,
If we wrapped the globe intensely with one hot electric
  breath,
'Twere but power within our tether, no new spirit-power
  comprising,
And in life we were not greater men, nor bolder men in
  death.'

She was patient with my talking; and I loved her, loved
  her, certes,
As I loved all heavenly objects, with uplifted eyes and hands;
As I loved pure inspirations, loved the graces, loved the
  virtues,
In a Love content with writing his own name on desert
  sands.

Or at least I thought so, purely! – thought no idiot Hope
  was raising
Any crown to crown Love's silence – silent Love that sat
  alone.
Out, alas! the stag is like me – he, that tries to go on grazing
With the great deep gun-wound in his neck, then reels
  with sudden moan.

It was thus I reeled. I told you that her hand had many
  suitors;

But she smiles them down imperially, as Venus did the
  waves,
And with such a gracious coldness, that they cannot press
  their futures
On the present of her courtesy, which yieldingly
  enslaves.

And this morning, as I sat alone within the inner
  chamber,
With the great saloon beyond it, lost in pleasant thought
  serene,
For I had been reading Camoëns, that poem you
  remember,
Which his lady's eyes are praised in, as the sweetest ever
  seen.

And the book lay open, and my thought flew from it,
  taking from it
A vibration and impulsion to an end beyond its own,
As the branch of a green osier, when a child would over-
  come it,
Springs up freely from his clasping and goes swinging in
  the sun.

As I mused I heard a murmur – it grew deep as it grew
  longer –
Speakers using earnest language – 'Lady Geraldine, you
  would!'
And I heard a voice that pleaded ever on, in accents
  stronger
As a sense of reason gave it power to make its rhetoric
  good.

Well I knew that voice; – it was an earl's, of soul that
  matched his station,
Soul completed into lordship, – might and right read on
  his brow;
Very finely courteous – far too proud to doubt his
  domination
Of the common people, he atones for grandeur by a bow.

High straight forehead, nose of eagle, cold blue eyes, of
  less expression
Than resistance, coldly casting off the looks of other
  men,
As steel, arrows, – unelastic lips, which seem to taste
  possession,
And be cautious lest the common air should injure or
  distrain.

For the rest, accomplished, upright, – aye, and standing
  by his order
With a bearing not ungraceful; fond of art and letters too;
Just a good man made a proud man, – as the sandy rocks
  that border
A wild coast, by circumstances, in a regnant ebb and flow.

Thus, I knew that voice – I heard it, and I could not help
  the hearkening.
In the room I stood up blindly, and my burning heart
  within
Seemed to seethe and fuse my senses, till they ran on all
  sides darkening,
And scorched, weighed, like melted metal round my feet
  that stood therein.

And that voice, I heard it pleading, for love's sake, for
  wealth, position,
For the sake of liberal uses, and great actions to be done –
And she interrupted gently, 'Nay, my lord, the old
  tradition
Of your Normans, by some worthier hand than mine is,
  should be won.'

'Ah, that white hand!' he said quickly, – and in his he
  either drew it
Or attempted – for with gravity and instance she replied,
'Nay, indeed, my lord, this talk is vain, and we had best
  eschew it,
And pass on, like friends, to other points less easy to
  decide.'

What he said again, I know not. It is likely that his
  trouble
Worked his pride up to the surface, for she answered in
  slow scorn,
'And your lordship judges rightly. Whom I marry, shall be
  noble,
Aye, and wealthy. I shall never blush to think how he was
  born.'

There, I maddened! her words stung me.
Life swept through me into fever,
And my soul sprang up astonished, sprang full-statured in
  an hour.
Know you what it is when anguish, with apocalyptic *never*,
To a Pythian height dilates you, – and despair sublimes to
  power?

From my brain the soul-wings budded, – waved a flame
about my body,
Whence conventions coiled to ashes. I felt self-drawn out,
as man,
From amalgamate false natures, and I saw the skies grow
ruddy
With the deepening feet of angels, and I knew what
spirits can.

I was mad – inspired – say either! (anguish worketh
inspiration)
Was a man, or beast – perhaps so, for the tiger roars,
when speared;
And I walked on, step by step, along the level of my
passion –
Oh my soul! and passed the doorway to her face, and
never feared.

He had left her, peradventure, when my footstep proved
my coming,
But for her – she half arose, then sat, grew scarlet and
grew pale.
Oh, she trembled! – 'tis so always with a worldly man or
woman
In the presence of true spirits – what else can they do but
quail?

Oh, she fluttered like a tame bird, in among its forest-
brothers
Far too strong for it; then drooping, bowed her face upon
her hands–

And I spake out wildly, fiercely, brutal truths of her and
others:
I, she planted in the desert, swathed her, windlike, with
my sands.

I plucked up her social fictions, bloody-rooted though
leaf-verdant, —
Trod them down with words of shaming, — all the purple
and the gold,
All the 'landed stakes' and lordships, all, that spirits pure
and ardent
Are cast out of love and honour because chancing not to hold.

'For myself I do not argue,' said I, 'though I love you,
madam,
But for better souls that nearer to the height of yours
have trod:
And this age shows, to my thinking, still more infidels to
Adam,
Than directly, by profession, simple infidels to God.

'Yet, O God,' I said, 'O grave,' I said, 'O mother's heart
and bosom,
With whom first and last are equal, saint and corpse and
little child!
We are fools to your deductions, in these figments of
heart-closing;
We are traitors to your causes, in these sympathies defiled.

'Learn more reverence, madam, not for rank or wealth —
that needs no learning,

That comes quickly — quick as sin does, aye, and culmi-
  nates to sin;
But for Adam's seed, MAN! Trust me, 'tis a clay above your
  scorning,
With God's image stamped upon it, and God's kindling
  breath within.

'What right have you, madam, gazing in your palace
  mirror daily,
Getting so by heart your beauty which all others must adore,
While you draw the golden ringlets down your fingers, to
  vow gaily
You will wed no man that's only good to God, and
  nothing more?

'Why, what right have you, made fair by that same God
  — the sweetest woman
Of all women He has fashioned — with your lovely
  spirit-face,
Which would seem too near to vanish if its smile were
  not so human,
And your voice of holy sweetness, turning common
  words to grace, —

'What right *can* you have, God's other works to scorn,
  despise, revile them
In the gross, as mere men, broadly — not as *noble* men,
  forsooth, —
As mere Pariahs of the outer world, forbidden to assoil
  them
In the hope of living, dying, near that sweetness of your
  mouth?

'Have you any answer, madam? If my spirit were less
  earthly,
If its instrument were gifted with a better silver string,
I would kneel down where I stand, and say — Behold me!
  I am worthy
Of thy loving, for I love thee! I am worthy as a king.

'As it is — your ermined pride, I swear, shall feel this
  stain upon her,
That I, poor, weak, tost with passion, scorned by me and
  you again,
Love you, madam, dare to love you — to my grief and
  your dishonour,
To my endless desolation, and your impotent disdain!'

More mad words like these — mere madness! friend, I
  need not write them fuller,
For I hear my hot soul dropping on the lines in showers
  of tears.
Oh, a woman! friend, a woman! why, a beast had scarce
  been duller
Than roar bestial loud complaints against the shining of
  the spheres.

But at last there came a pause. I stood all vibrating with
  thunder
Which my soul had used. The silence drew her face up
  like a call.
Could you guess what word she uttered? She looked up,
  as if in wonder,
With tears beaded on her lashes, and said 'Bertram!' — it
  was all.

If she had cursed me, and she might have − or if even,
   with queenly bearing
Which at need is used by women, she had risen up and
   said,
'Sir, you are my guest, and therefore I have given you a
   full hearing'
Now, beseech you, choose a name exacting somewhat
   less, instead!' −

I had borne it! but that 'Bertram' − why, it lies there on
   the paper
A mere word, without her accent, − and you cannot
   judge the weight
Of the calm which crushed my passion: I seemed
   drowning in a vapour, − ·
And her gentleness destroyed me whom her scorn made
   desolate.

So, struck backward and exhausted by that inward flow of
   passion
Which had rushed on, sparing nothing, into forms of
   abstract truth,
By a logic agonising through unseemly demonstration,
And by youth's own anguish turning grimly grey the
   hairs of youth, −

By the sense accursed and instant, that if even I spake
   wisely
I spake basely − using truth, if what I spake indeed was
   true,
To avenge wrong on a woman − her, who sat there
   weighing nicely

A poor manhood's worth, found guilty of such deeds as I
    could do! –

By such wrong and woe exhausted – what
I suffered and occasioned, –
As a wild horse through a city runs with lightning in his
    eyes,
And then dashing at a church's cold and passive wall,
    impassioned,
Strikes the death into his burning brain, and blindly drops
    and dies –

So I fell, struck down before her! do you blame me,
    friend, for weakness?
'Twas my strength of passion slew me! – fell before her
    like a stone.
Fast the dreadful world rolled from me on its roaring
    wheels of blackness –
When the light came, I was lying in this chamber, and
    alone.

Oh, of course, she charged her lacqueys to bear out the
    sickly burden,
And to cast it from her scornful sight – but not *beyond* the
    gate;
She is too kind to be cruel, and too haughty not to
    pardon
Such a man as I – 'twere something to be level to her
    hate.

But for me – you now are conscious why, my friend, I
    write this letter,

How my life is read all backward, and the charm of life
   undone:
I shall leave her house at dawn; I would tonight, if I were
   better —
And I charge my soul to hold my body strengthened for
   the sun.

When the sun has dyed the oriel, I depart, with no last
   gazes,
No weak moanings (one word only, left in writing for
   her hands),
Out of reach of all derision, and some unavailing
   praises,
To make front against this anguish in the far and foreign
   lands.

Blame me not. I would not squander life in grief — I am
   abstemious:
I but nurse my spirit's falcon, that its wing may soar again.
There's no room for tears of weakness in the blind eyes of
   a Phemius!
Into work the poet kneads them, — and he does not die
   till then.

Conclusion

Bertram finished the last pages, while along the silence ever
Still in hot and heavy splashes fell the tears on every leaf:
Having ended he leans backward in his chair, with lips
   that quiver
From the deep unspoken, aye, and deep unwritten
   thoughts of grief.

Soh! how still the lady standeth! 'T is a dream — a dream
  of mercies!
'Twixt the purple lattice-curtains, how she standeth still
  and pale!
'T is a vision, sure, of mercies, sent to soften his self-
  curses —
Sent to sweep a patient quiet o'er the tossing of his wail.

 'Eyes,' he said, 'now throbbing through me! are ye eyes
  that did undo me?
Shining eyes, like antique jewels set in Parian statue-stone!
Underneath that calm white forehead, are ye ever burning
  torrid
O'er the desolate sand-desert of my heart and life
  undone?'

With a murmurous stir uncertain, in the air the purple
  curtain
Swelleth in and swelleth out around her motionless pale
  brows,
While the gliding of the river sends a rippling noise for
  ever
Through the open casement whitened by the moonlight's
  slant repose.

Said he — 'Vision of a lady! stand there silent, stand there
  steady!
Now I see it plainly, plainly; now I cannot hope or doubt
  —
There, the brows of mild repression — there, the lips of
  silent passion,
Curvèd like an archer's bow to send the bitter arrows out.'

Ever, evermore the while in a slow silence she kept
  smiling,
And approached him slowly, slowly, in a gliding measured
  pace;
With her two white hands extended, as if praying one
  offended,
And a look of supplication, gazing earnest in his face.

Said he – 'Wake me by no gesture, – sound of breath, or
  stir of vesture!
Let the blessèd apparition melt not yet to its divine!
No approaching – hush, no breathing! or my heart must
  swoon to death in
The too utter life thou bringest, O thou dream of
  Geraldine!'

Ever, evermore the while in a slow silence she kept
  smiling –
But the tears ran over lightly from her eyes and tenderly:
  –
'Dost thou, Bertram, truly love me? Is no woman far
  above me
Found more worthy of thy poet heart than such a one as
  I?'

Said he – 'I would dream so ever, like the flowing of that
  river,
Flowing ever in a shadow greenly onward to the sea!
So, thou vision of all sweetness – princely to a full
  completeness –
Would my heart and life flow onward – deathward –
  through this dream of THEE!'

Ever, evermore the while in a slow silence she kept
  smiling,
While the silver tears ran faster down the blushing of her
  cheeks;
Then with both her hands enfolding both of his, she
  softly told him,
'Bertram, if I say I love thee, ... 't is the vision only
  speaks.'

Softened, quickened to adore her, on his knee he fell
  before her –
And she whispered low in triumph, 'It shall be as I have
  sworn!
Very rich he is in virtues, – very noble – noble, certes;
And I shall not blush in knowing that men call him lowly
  born.'

The Lady's Yes

'Yes!' I answered you last night;
  'No!' this morning, Sir, I say.
Colours, seen by candle-light,
  Will not look the same by day.

When the viols played their best,
  Lamps above, and laughs below,
Love me sounded like a jest,
  Fit for *yes*, or fit for *no*!

Call me false, or call me free –
  Vow, whatever light may shine,
No man on your face shall see
  Any grief, for change on mine.

Yet the sin is on us both;
  Time to dance is not to woo;
Wooing light makes fickle troth,
  Scorn of *me* recoils on *you*.

Learn to win a lady's faith
  Nobly, as the thing is high,
Bravely, as for life and death,
  With a loyal gravity.

Lead her from the festive boards,
  Point her to the starry skies,
Guard her, by your truthful words,
  Pure from courtship's flatteries.

By your truth she shall be true,
  Ever true, as wives of yore;
And her *yes*, once said to you,
  SHALL be Yes for evermore.

Catarina to Camoëns

*Dying in his absence abroad, and referring to the poem in which
he recorded the sweetness of her eyes*

⁊

On the door you will not enter,
  I have gazed too long – adieu!
Hope withdraws her peradventure –
  Death is near me, – and not you.
    Come, O lover,
    Close and cover
These poor eyes, you called, I ween,
'Sweetest eyes, were ever seen.'

When I heard you sing that burden
  In my vernal days and bowers,
Other praises disregarding,
  I but hearkened that of yours –
    Only saying
    In heart-playing,
'Blessed eyes mine eyes have been,
If the sweetest, HIS have seen!'

But all changes. At this vesper,
  Cold the sun shines down the door.
If you stood there, would you whisper
  'Love, I love you,' as before, –
    Death pervading
    Now, and shading

Eyes you sang of, that yestreen,
As the sweetest ever seen?

Yes. I think, were you beside them,
   Near the bed I die upon, –
Though their beauty you denied them,
   As you stood there, looking down,
      You would truly
      Call them duly,
For the love's sake found therein, –
'Sweetest eyes, were ever seen.'

And if you looked down upon them,
   And if they looked up to you,
All the light which has foregone them
   Would be gathered back anew:
      They would truly
      Be as duly
Love-transformed to beauty's sheen, –
'Sweetest eyes, were ever seen.'

But, ah me! you only see me,
   In your thoughts of loving man,
Smiling soft perhaps and dreamy
   Through the wavings of my fan, –
      And unweeting
      Go repeating,
In your reverie serene,
'Sweetest eyes, were ever seen.'

While my spirit leans and reaches
  From my body still and pale,
Fain to hear what tender speech is
  In your love to help my bale –
    O my poet,
    Come and show it!
Come, of latest love, to glean
'Sweetest eyes, were ever seen.'

O my poet, O my prophet,
  When you praised their sweetness so,
Did you think, in singing of it,
  That it might be near to go?
    Had you fancies
    From their glances,
That the grave would quickly screen
'Sweetest eyes, were ever seen'?

No reply! The fountain's warble
  In the courtyard sounds alone.
As the water to the marble
  So my heart falls with a moan
    From love-sighing
    To this dying.
Death forerunneth Love to win
'Sweetest eyes, were ever seen.'

Will you come? When I'm departed
  Where all sweetnesses are hid;
Where thy voice, my tender-hearted,
  Will not lift up either lid.
    Cry, O lover,

Love is over!
Cry, beneath the cypress green —
'Sweetest eyes, were ever seen.'

When the angelus is ringing,
  Near the convent will you walk,
And recall the choral singing
  Which brought angels down our
    talk?
    Spirit-shriven
    I viewed Heaven,
Till you smiled — 'Is earth unclean,
Sweetest eyes, were ever seen?'

When beneath the palace-lattice,
  You ride slow as you have done,
And you see a face there — that is
  Not the old familiar one, —
    Will you oftly
    Murmur softly,
'Here ye watched me morn and
  e'en,
Sweetest eyes, were ever seen?'

When the palace-ladies, sitting
  Round your gittern, shall have said,
'Poet, sing those verses written
  For the lady who is dead,'
    Will you tremble
    Yet dissemble, —
Or sing hoarse, with tears between,
'Sweetest eyes, were ever seen'?

'Sweetest eyes!' how sweet in flowings
  The repeated cadence is!
Though you sang a hundred poems,
  Still the best one would be this.
    I can hear it
    'Twixt my spirit
And the earth-noise intervene –
'Sweetest eyes, were ever seen!'

But the priest waits for the praying,
  And the choir are on their knees,
And the soul must pass away in
  Strains more solemn-high than these.
    Miserere
    For the weary!
Oh, no longer for Catrine,
'Sweetest eyes, were ever seen!'

Keep my ribbon, take and keep it
  (I have loosed it from my hair),
Feeling, while you overweep it,
  Not alone in your despair,
    Since with saintly
    Watch unfaintly
Out of heaven shall o'er you lean
'Sweetest eyes, were ever seen.'

But – but *now* – yet unremovèd
  Up to Heaven, they glisten fast.
You may cast away, Belovèd,
  In your future all my past.
    Such old phrases

May be praises
For some fairer bosom-queen –
'Sweetest eyes, were ever seen!'

Eyes of mine, what are ye doing?
   Faithless, faithless, – praised amiss
If a tear be of your showing,
   Dropt for any hope of HIS!
      Death has boldness
      Besides coldness,
If unworthy tears demean
'Sweetest eyes, were ever seen.'

I will look out to his future;
   I will bless it till it shine.
Should he ever be a suitor
   Unto sweeter eyes than mine,
      Sunshine gild them,
      Angels shield them,
Whatsoever eyes terrene
Be the sweetest, HIS have seen!

A Rhapsody of Life's Progress

Fill all the stops of life with tuneful breath.

CORNELIUS MATHEWS,
Poems of Man

∂

We are borne into life – it is sweet, it is strange.
We lie still on the knee of a mild Mystery,
  Which smiles with a change!
But we doubt not of changes, we know not of spaces,
The Heavens seem as near as our own mother's face is,
And we think we could touch all the stars that we see;
And the milk of our mother is white on our mouth;
And, with small childish hands, we are turning around
The apple of Life which another has found;
It is warm with our touch, not with sun of the south,
And we count, as we turn it, the red side for four.
    O Life, O Beyond,
  Thou art sweet, thou art strange evermore!

Then all things look strange in the pure golden ether:
We walk through the gardens with hands linked together,
  And the lilies look large as the trees;
And as loud as the birds sing the bloom-loving bees,
And the birds sing like angels, so mystical-fine,
And the cedars are brushing the archangels' feet,
And time is eternity, love is divine,
  And the world is complete.
Now, God bless the child, – father, mother, respond!

O Life, O Beyond,
Thou art strange, thou art sweet.

Then we leap on the earth with the armour of youth,
    And the earth rings again,
And we breathe out, 'O Beauty,' – we cry out, 'O truth,'
And the bloom of our lips drops with wine,
And our blood runs amazed 'neath the calm hyaline,
The earth cleaves to the foot, the sun burns to the brain, –
What is this exultation? and what this despair? –
The strong pleasure is smiting the nerves into pain,
And we drop from the Fair as we climb to the Fair,
    And we lie in a trance at its feet;
And the breath of an angel cold-piercing the air
    Breathes fresh on our faces in swoon,
And we think him so near he is this side the sun,
And we wake to a whisper self-murmured and fond,
    O Life, O Beyond,
    Thou art strange, thou art sweet!

And the winds and the waters in pastoral measures
Go winding around us, with roll upon roll,
Till the soul lies within in a circle of pleasures
Which hideth the soul.
And we run with the stag, and we leap with the horse,
And we swim with the fish through the broad watercourse,
And we strike with the falcon, and hunt with the hound,
And the joy which is in us flies out by a wound.
And we shout so aloud, 'We exult, we rejoice,'
That we lose the low moan of our brothers around;
And we shout so adeep down creation's profound,
    We are deaf to God's voice.

And we bind the rose-garland on forehead and ears
    Yet we are not ashamed,
And the dew of the roses that runneth unblamed
  Down our cheeks, is not taken for tears.
Help us, God, trust us, man! love us, woman! 'I hold
Thy small head in my hands, – with its grapelets of gold
Growing bright through my fingers, – like altar for oath,
'Neath the vast golden spaces like witnessing faces
That watch the eternity strong in the troth –
  I love thee, I leave thee,
  Live for thee, die for thee!
  I prove thee, deceive thee,
  Undo evermore thee!
Help me, God! slay me, man! – one is mourning for both.'
And we stand up, though young, near the funeral-sheet
Which covers the Caesar and old Pharamond,
And death is so nigh us, life cools from its heat.
    O Life, O Beyond,
  Art thou fair, – art thou sweet?

Then we act to a purpose – we spring up erect:
We will tame the wild mouths of the wilderness-steeds,
We will plough up the deep in the ships double-decked,
We will build the great cities, and do the great deeds,
Strike the steel upon steel, strike the soul upon soul,
Strike the dole on the weal, overcoming the dole.
Let the cloud meet the cloud in a grand thunder-roll!
'While the eagle of Thought rides the tempest in scorn,
Who cares if the lightning is burning the corn?
  Let us sit on the thrones
  In a purple sublimity,
  And grind down men's bones

To a pale unanimity.
Speed me, God! – serve me, man! – I am god over men;
When I speak in my cloud, none shall answer again,
  'Neath the stripe and the bond,
    Lie and mourn at my feet!' –
  O Life, O Beyond,
    Thou art strange, thou art sweet!

Then we grow into thought, – and with inward ascensions
  Touch the bounds of our Being.
We lie in the dark here, swathed doubly around
With our sensual relations and social conventions,
Yet are 'ware of a sight, yet are 'ware of a sound
    Beyond Hearing and Seeing, –
Are aware that a Hades rolls deep on all sides
    With its infinite tides
About and above us, – until the strong arch
Of our life creaks and bends as if ready for falling,
And through the dim rolling we hear the sweet calling
Of spirits that speak in a soft under-tongue
  The sense of the mystical march.
And we cry to them softly, 'Come nearer, come nearer,
And lift up the lap of this Dark, and speak clearer,
  And teach us the song that ye sung!'
And we smile in our thought as they answer or no,
For to dream of a sweetness is sweet as to know.
  Wonders breathe in our face
    And we ask not their name;
    Love takes all the blame
  Of the world's prison-place.
And we sing back the songs as we guess them, aloud;
And we send up the lark of our music that cuts

Untired through the cloud,
To beat with its wings at the lattice Heaven shuts;
Yet the angels look down and the mortals look up
    As the little wings beat,
And the poet is blessed with their pity or hope.
'Twixt the heavens and the earth can a poet despond?
    O Life, O Beyond,
Thou art strange, thou art sweet!

Then we wring from our souls their applicative strength,
And bend to the cord the strong bow of our ken,
And bringing our lives to the level of others
Hold the cup we have filled, to their uses at length.
'Help me, God! love me, man! I am man among men,
    And my life is a pledge
    Of the ease of another's!'
From the fire and the water we drive out the steam
With a rush and a roar and the speed of a dream;
And the car without horses, the car without wings,
    Roars onward and flies
    On its grey iron edge,
'Neath the heat of a Thought sitting still in our eyes:
And our hand knots in air, with the bridge that it flings,
Two peaks far disrupted by ocean and skies,
And, lifting a fold of the smooth-flowing Thames,
Draws under the world with its turmoils and pothers,
While the swans float on softly, untouched in their calms
By humanity's hum at the root of the springs.
And with reachings of Thought we reach down to the
    deeps
    Of the souls of our brothers, –
We teach them full words with our slow-moving lips,

'God,' 'Liberty,' 'Truth,' – which they hearken and think
And work into harmony, link upon link,
Till the silver meets round the earth gelid and dense,
Shedding sparks of electric responding intense
    On the dark of eclipse.
Then we hear through the silence and glory afar,
    As from shores of a star
In aphelion, the new generations that cry
Disenthralled by our voice to harmonious reply,
    'God,' 'Liberty,' 'Truth!'
    We are glorious forsooth –
    And our name has a seat,
Though the shroud should be donned.
    O Life, O Beyond,
Thou art strange, thou art sweet!

Help me, God – help me, man! I am low, I am weak –
Death loosens my sinews and creeps in my veins:
My body is cleft by these wedges of pains
    From my spirit's serene,
And I feel the externe and insensate creep in
    On my organised clay.
    I sob not, nor shriek,
    Yet I faint fast away!
I am strong in the spirit, – deep-thoughted, clear-eyed, –
I could walk, step for step, with an angel beside,
    On the heaven-heights of truth.
    Oh, the soul keeps its youth,
But the body faints sore, it is tried in the race,
It sinks from the chariot ere reaching the goal,
    It is weak, it is cold,
    The rein drops from its hold –

It sinks back, with the death in its face.
  On, chariot – on, soul,
  Ye are all the more fleet –
  Be alone at the goal
  Of the strange and the sweet!

Love us, God, love us, man! we believe, we achieve –
  Let us love, let us live,
  For the acts correspond;
  We are glorious – and DIE:
And again on the knee of a mild Mystery
  That smiles with a change,
    Here we lie.
    O DEATH, O BEYOND,
Thou art sweet, thou art strange!

Work and Contemplation

The woman singeth at her spinning-wheel
A pleasant chant, ballad or barcarole:
She thinketh of her song, upon the whole,
Far more than of her flax; and yet the reel
Is full, and artfully her fingers feel
With quick adjustment, provident control,
The lines – too subtly twisted to unroll,
Out to a perfect thread. I hence appeal
To the dear Christian Church – that we may do
Our Father's business in these temples mirk,
Thus swift and steadfast, – thus, intent and strong;
While, thus, apart from toil, our souls pursue
Some high, calm, spheric tune, and prove our work
The better for the sweetness of our song.

Patience Taught by Nature

'O dreary life,' we cry, 'O dreary life!'
And still the generations of the birds
Sing through our sighing, and the flocks and herds
Serenely live while we are keeping strife
With Heaven's true purpose in us, as a knife
Against which we may struggle! ocean girds
Unslackened the dry land, savannah-swards
Unweary sweep, – hills watch, unworn; and rife
Meek leaves drop yearly from the forest-trees,
To show above the unwasted stars that pass
In their old glory. O thou God of old,
Grant me some smaller grace than comes to these! –
But so much patience as a blade of grass
Grows by, contented through the heat and cold.

To George Sand

A DESIRE

Thou large-brained woman and large-hearted man,
Self-called George Sand! whose soul, amid the lions
Of thy tumultuous senses, moans defiance,
And answers roar for roar, as spirits can!
I would some mild miraculous thunder ran
Above the applauded circus, in appliance
Of thine own nobler nature's strength and science,
Drawing two pinions, white as wings of swan,
From thy strong shoulders, to amaze the place
With holier light! that thou to woman's claim,
And man's, mightst join beside the angel's grace
Of a pure genius sanctified from blame, –
Till child and maiden pressed to thine embrace,
To kiss upon thy lips a stainless fame.

To George Sand

A RECOGNITION

True genius, but true woman! dost deny
Thy woman's nature with a manly scorn,
And break away the gauds and armlets worn
By weaker women in captivity?
Ah, vain denial! that revolted cry
Is sobbed in by a woman's voice forlorn! –
Thy woman's hair, my sister, all unshorn,
Floats back dishevelled strength in agony,
Disproving thy man's name! and while before
The world thou burnest in a poet-fire,
We see thy woman-heart beat evermore
Through the large flame. Beat purer, heart, and higher,
Till God unsex thee on the heavenly shore,
Where unincarnate spirits purely aspire!

The Soul's Expression

With stammering lips and insufficient sound
I strive and struggle to deliver right
That music of my nature, day and night
With dream and thought and feeling interwound,
And inly answering all the senses round
With octaves of a mystic depth and height
Which step out grandly to the infinite
From the dark edges of the sensual ground!
This song of soul I struggle to outbear
Through portals of the sense, sublime and whole,
And utter all myself into the air.
But if I did it, − as the thunder-roll
Breaks its own cloud, my flesh would perish there,
Before that dread apocalypse of soul.

The House of Clouds

I would build a cloudy House
  For my thoughts to live in,
When for earth too fancy-loose,
  And too low for heaven.
Hush! I talk my dream aloud;
  I build it bright to see, –
I build it on the moonlit cloud,
  To which I looked with thee.

Cloud-walls of the morning's grey,
  Faced with amber column,
Crowned with crimson cupola
  From a sunset solemn:
May mists, for the casements, fetch,
  Pale and glimmering,
With a sunbeam hid in each,
  And a smell of spring.

Build the entrance high and proud,
  Darkening and then brightening,
If a riven thunder-cloud,
  Veined by the lightning:
Use one with an iris-stain,
  For the door within,
Turning to a sound like rain
  As I enter in.

Build a spacious hall thereby,
  Boldly, never fearing;
Use the blue place of the sky

Which the wind is clearing;
Branched with corridors sublime,
　Flecked with winding stairs,
Such as children wish to climb,
　Following their own prayers.

In the mutest of the house,
　I will have my chamber:
Silence at the door shall use
　Evening's light of amber;
Solemnising every mood,
　Softening in degree,
Turning sadness into good,
　As I turn the key.

Be my chamber tapestried
　With the showers of summer,
Close, but soundless, – glorified
　When the sunbeams come here;
Wandering harpers, harping on
　Waters stringed for such, –
Drawing colour, for a tune,
　With a vibrant touch.

Bring a shadow green and still
　From the chestnut forest,
Bring a purple from the hill,
　When the heat is sorest;
Spread them out from wall to wall,
　Carpet-wove around,
Whereupon the foot shall fall
　In light instead of sound.

Bring fantasque cloudlets home
　From the noontide zenith
Ranged for sculptures round the room,
　Named as Fancy weeneth.
Some be Junos, without eyes,
　Naiads, without sources;
Some be birds of paradise,
　Some, Olympian horses.

Bring the dews the birds shake off,
　Waking in the hedges, –
Those too, perfumed for a proof,
　From the lilies' edges,
From our England's field and moor;
　Bring them calm and white in,
Whence to form a mirror pure
　For Love's self-delighting.

Bring a grey cloud from the east
　Where the lark is singing
(Something of the song at least
　Unlost in the bringing):
That shall be a morning chair
　Poet-dream may sit in,
When it leans out on the air,
　Unrimed and unwritten.

Bring the red cloud from the sun!
　While he sinketh, catch it:
That shall be a couch, – with one
　Sidelong star to watch it, –
Fit for Poet's finest thought

At the curfew-sounding;
Things unseen being nearer brought
    Than the seen, around him.

Poet's thought,—-not poet's sigh – .
    'Las, they come together!
Cloudy walls divide and fly,
    As in April weather!
Cupola and column proud,
    Structure bright to see,
Gone! except that moonlit cloud
    To which I looked with thee!

Let them. Wipe such visionings
    From the fancy's cartel:
Love secures some fairer things,
    Dowered with his immortal.
The sun may darken, heaven be bowed,
    But still, unchanged shall be, –
Here, in my soul, –that moonlit cloud,
    To which I looked with THEE!

The Prisoner

I count the dismal time by months and years,
Since last I felt the green sward under foot,
And the great breath of all things summer-mute
Met mine upon my lips. Now earth appears
As strange to me as dreams of distant spheres,
Or thoughts of Heaven we weep at. Nature's lute
Sounds on behind this door so closely shut,
A strange, wild music to the prisoner's ears,
Dilated by the distance, till the brain
Grows dim with fancies which it feels too fine
While ever, with a visionary pain,
Past the precluded senses, sweep and shine
Streams, forests, glades, – and many a golden train
Of sunlit hills, transfigured to Divine.

The Prospect

Methinks we do as fretful children do,
Leaning their faces on the window-pane
To sigh the glass dim with their own breath's stain,
And shut the sky and landscape from their view.
And, thus, alas! since God the maker drew
A mystic separation 'twixt those twain,
The life beyond us, and our souls in pain,
We miss the prospect which we are called unto
By grief we are fools to use. Be still and strong,
O man, my brother! hold thy sobbing breath,
And keep thy soul's large windows pure from wrong, –
That so, as life's appointment issueth,
Thy vision may be clear to watch along
The sunset consummation-lights of death.

Tears

Thank God, bless God, all ye who suffer not
More grief than ye can weep for. That is well –
That is light grieving! lighter, none befell
Since Adam forfeited the primal lot.
Tears! what are tears? The babe weeps in its cot,
The mother singing, – at her marriage bell
The bride weeps, – and before the oracle
Of high-faned hills, the poet has forgot
Such moisture on his cheeks. Thank God for grace,
Ye who weep only! If, as some have done,
Ye grope tear-blinded in a desert place
And touch but tombs, – look up! those tears will run
Soon in long rivers down the lifted face,
And leave the vision clear for stars and sun.

Comfort

Speak low to me, my Saviour, low and sweet
From out the hallelujahs, sweet and low,
Lest I should fear and fall, and miss Thee so
Who art not missed by any that entreat.
Speak to me as Mary at Thy feet!
And if no precious gums my hands bestow,
Let my tears drop like amber, while I go
In reach of Thy divinest voice complete
In humanest affection – thus, in sooth,
To lose the sense of losing! As a child.
Whose song-bird seeks the woods for evermore,
Is sung to instead by mother's mouth,
Till, sinking on her breast, love-reconciled,
He sleeps the faster that he wept before.

Discontent

Light human nature is too lightly tost
And ruffled without cause, – complaining on,
Restless with rest – until, being overthrown,
It learneth to lie quiet. Let a frost
Or a small wasp have crept to the innermost
Of our ripe peach, or let the wilful sun
Shine westward of our window, – straight we run
A furlong's sigh, as if the world were lost.
But what time through the heart and through the brain
God hath transfixed us, – we, so moved before,
Attain to a calm. Aye, shouldering weights of pain,
We anchor in deep waters, safe from shore,
And hear, submissive, o'er the stormy main,
God's chartered judgments walk for evermore.

Farewells from Paradise

River-spirits
Hark! the flow of the four rivers –
  Hark the flow!
How the silence round you shivers,
While our voices through it go,
  Cold and clear.

A softer voice
Think a little, while ye hear,
  Of the banks
Where the willows and the deer
Crowd in intermingled ranks,
As if all would drink at once
Where the living water runs! –
Of the fishes' golden edges
Flashing in and out the sedges;
Of the swans on silver thrones,
Floating down the winding streams
With impassive eyes turned shoreward
And a chant of undertones, –
And the lotus leaning forward
To help them into dreams.
  Fare ye well, farewell!
The river-sounds, no longer audible,
  Expire at Eden's door.
  Each footstep of your treading
Treads out some murmur which ye heard
  before.
Farewell! the streams of Eden
Ye shall hear nevermore!

Bird-spirit

I am the nearest nightingale
That singeth in Eden after you;
And I am singing loud and true,
And sweet, — I do not fail.
I sit upon a cypress bough,
Close to the gate, and I fling my song
   Over the gate and through the mail
Of the warden angels marshall'd strong, —
Over the gate and after you!
And the warden angels let it pass,
Because the poor brown bird, alas,
   Sings in the garden, sweet and true.
And I build my song of high pure notes,
Note over note, height over height,
Till I strike the arch of the Infinite,
And I bridge abysmal agonies
With strong, clear calms of harmonies, —
And something abides, and something floats,
In the song which I sing after you.
   Fare ye well, farewell!
The creature-sounds, no longer audible,
   Expire at Eden's door.
   Each footstep of your treading
Treads out some cadence which ye heard before,
   Farewell! the birds of Eden
   Ye shall hear nevermore!

Sonnets from the Portuguese

I

I thought once how Theocritus had sung
Of the sweet years, the dear and wished-for years,
Who each one in a gracious hand appears
To bear a gift for mortals, old or young:
And, as I mused it in his antique tongue,
I saw, in gradual vision through my tears,
The sweet, sad years, the melancholy years,
Those of my own life, who by turns had flung
A shadow across me. Straightway I was 'ware,
So weeping, how a mystic Shape did move
Behind me, and drew me backward by the hair,
And a voice said in mastery while I strove, ...
'Guess now who holds thee!' – 'Death,' I said. But, there,
The silver answer rang ... 'Not Death, but Love.'

II

But only three in all God's universe
Have heard this word thou hast said, – Himself, beside
Thee speaking, and me listening! and replied
One of us ... that was God, ... and laid the curse
So darkly on my eyelids, as to amerce
My sight from seeing thee, – that if I had died,
The deathweights, placed there, would have signified
Less absolute exclusion. 'Nay' is worse
From God than from all others, O my friend!
Men could not part us with their worldly jars,
Nor the seas change us, nor the tempests bend;
Our hands would touch for all the mountain-bars, –
And, heaven being rolled between us at the end,
We should but vow the faster for the stars.

III

Unlike are we, unlike, O princely Heart!
Unlike our uses and our destinies.
Our ministering two angels look surprise
On one another, as they strike athwart
Their wings in passing. Thou, bethink thee, art
A guest for queens to social pageantries,
With gages from a hundred brighter eyes
Than tears even can make mine, to play thy part
Of chief musician. What hast thou to do
With looking from the lattice-lights at me,
A poor, tired, wandering singer, ... singing through
The dark, and leaning up a cypress tree?
The chrism is on thine head, – on mine, the dew, –
And Death must dig the level where these agree.

IV

Thou hast thy calling to some palace-floor,
Most gracious singer of high poems! where
The dancers will break footing, from the care
Of watching up thy pregnant lips for more.
And dost thou lift this house's latch too poor
For hand of thine? and canst thou think and bear
To let thy music drop here unaware
In folds of golden fullness at my door?
Look up and see the casement broken in,
The bats and owlets builders in the roof!
My cricket chirps against thy mandolin.
Hush, call no echo up in further proof
Of desolation! there's a voice within
That weeps ... as thou must sing ... alone, aloof.

V

I lift my heavy heart up solemnly,
As once Electra her sepulchral urn,
And, looking in thine eyes, I over-turn
The ashes at thy feet. Behold and see
What a great heap of grief lay hid in me,
And how the red wild sparkles dimly burn
Through the ashen greyness. If thy foot in scorn
Could tread them out to darkness utterly,
It might be well perhaps. But if instead
Thou wait beside me for the wind to blow
The grey dust up, … those laurels on thine head,
O my Belovèd, will not shield thee so,
That none of all the fires shall scorch and shred
The hair beneath. Stand further off then! go.

VI

Go from me. Yet I feel that I shall stand
Henceforward in thy shadow. Nevermore
Alone upon the threshold of my door
Of individual life, I shall command
The uses of my soul, nor lift my hand
Serenely in the sunshine as before,
Without the sense of that which I forbore, …
Thy touch upon the palm. The widest land
Doom takes to part us, leaves thy heart in mine
With pulses that beat double. What I do
And what I dream include thee, as the wine
Must taste of its own grapes. And when I sue
God for myself, He hears that name of thine,
And sees within my eyes the tears of two.

VII

The face of all the world is changed, I think,
Since first I heard the footsteps of thy soul
Move still, oh, still, beside me, as they stole
Betwixt me and the dreadful outer brink
Of obvious death, where I, who thought to sink,
Was caught up into love, and taught the whole
Of life in a new rhythm. The cup of dole
God gave for baptism, I am fain to drink,
And praise its sweetness, Sweet, with thee anear.
The names of country, heaven, are changed away
For where thou art or shalt be, there or here;
And this ... this lute and song ... loved yesterday,
(The singing angels know) are only dear,
Because thy name moves right in what they say.

VIII

What can I give thee back, O liberal
And princely giver, who hast brought the gold
And purple of thine heart, unstained, untold,
And laid them on the outside of the wall
For such as I to take or leave withal,
In unexpected largesse? am I cold,
Ungrateful, that for these most manifold
High gifts, I render nothing back at all?
Not so; not cold, – but very poor instead.
Ask God who knows. For frequent tears have run
The colours from my life, and left so dead
And pale a stuff, it were not fitly done
To give the same as pillow to thy head.
Go farther! let it serve to trample on.

IX

Can it be right to give what I can give?
To let thee sit beneath the fall of tears
As salt as mine, and hear the sighing years
Re-sighing on my lips renunciative
Through those infrequent smiles which fail to live
For all thy adjurations? O my fears,
That this can scarce be right! We are not peers,
So to be lovers; and I own, and grieve,
That givers of such gifts as mine are, must
Be counted with the ungenerous. Out, alas!
I will not soil thy purple with my dust,
Nor breathe my poison on thy Venice-glass,
Nor give thee any love ... which were unjust.
Beloved, I only love thee! let it pass.

X

Yet, love, mere love, is beautiful indeed
And worthy of acceptation. Fire is bright,
Let temple burn, or flax. An equal light
Leaps in the flame from cedar-plank or weed.
And love is fire; and when I say at need
I love thee ... mark! ... *I love thee* ... in thy sight
I stand transfigured, glorified aright,
With conscience of the new rays that proceed
Out of my face toward thine. There's nothing low
In love, when love the lowest: meanest creatures
Who love God, God accepts while loving so.
And what I *feel*, across the inferior features
Of what I *am*, doth flash itself, and show
How that great work of Love enhances Nature's.

XI

And therefore if to love can be desert,
I am not all unworthy. Cheeks as pale
As these you see, and trembling knees that fail
To bear the burden of a heavy heart, –
This weary minstrel-life that once was girt
To climb Aornus, and can scarce avail
To pipe now 'gainst the valley nightingale
A melancholy music, – why advert
To these things? O Belovèd, it is plain
I am not of thy worth nor for thy place!
And yet, because I love thee, I obtain
From that same love this vindicating grace,
To live on still in love, and yet in vain, ...
To bless thee, yet renounce thee to thy face.

XII

Indeed this very love which is my boast,
And which, when rising up from breast to brow,
Doth crown me with a ruby large enow
To draw men's eyes and prove the inner cost, ...
This love even, all my worth, to the uttermost,
I should not love withal, unless that thou
Hadst set me an example, shown me how,
When first thine earnest eyes with mine were crossed,
And love called love. And thus, I cannot speak
Of love even, as a good thing of my own.
Thy soul hath snatched up mine all faint and weak,
And placed it by thee on a golden throne, –
And that I love (O soul, we must be meek!)
Is by thee only, whom I love alone.

XIII

And wilt thou have me fashion into speech
The love I bear thee, finding words enough,
And hold the torch out, while the winds are rough,
Between our faces, to cast light on each? –
I drop it at thy feet. I cannot teach
My hand to hold my spirits so far off
From myself … me … that I should bring thee proof
In words, of love hid in me out of reach.
Nay, let the silence of my womanhood
Commend my woman-love to thy belief, –
Seeing that I stand unwon, however wooed,
And rend the garment of my life, in brief,
By a most dauntless, voiceless fortitude,
Lest one touch of this heart convey its grief.

XIV

If thou must love me, let it be for nought
Except for love's sake only. Do not say
'I love her for her smile … her look … her way
Of speaking gently … for a trick of thought
That falls in well with mine, and certes brought
A sense of pleasant ease on such a day' –
For these things in themselves, Belovèd, may
Be changed, or change for thee, – and love, so wrought,
May be unwrought so. Neither love me for
Thine own dear pity's wiping my cheeks dry, –
A creature might forget to weep, who bore
Thy comfort long, and lose thy love thereby!
But love me for love's sake, that evermore
Thou mayst love on, through love's eternity.

XV

Accuse me not, beseech thee, that I wear
Too calm and sad a face in front of thine;
For we two look two ways, and cannot shine
With the same sunlight on our brow and hair.
On me thou lookest with no doubting care,
As on a bee shut in a crystalline, —
Since sorrow hath shut me safe in love's divine,
And to spread wing and fly in the outer air
Were most impossible failure, if I strove
To fail so. But I look on thee ... on thee ...
Beholding, besides love, the end of love,
Hearing oblivion beyond memory!
As one who sits and gazes from above,
Over the rivers to the bitter sea.

XVI

And yet, because thou overcomest so,
Because thou art more noble and like a king,
Thou canst prevail against my fears and fling
Thy purple round me, till my heart shall grow
Too close against thine heart henceforth to know
How it shook when alone. Why, conquering
May prove as lordly and complete a thing
In lifting upward, as in crushing low!
And as a vanquished soldier yields his sword
To one who lifts him from the bloody earth —
Even so, Belovèd, I at last record,
Here ends my strife. If thou invite me forth,
I rise above abasement at the word.
Make thy love larger to enlarge my worth.

XVII

My poet, thou canst touch on all the notes
God set between His After and Before,
And strike up and strike off the general roar
Of the rushing worlds, a melody that floats
In a serene air purely. Antidotes
Of medicated music, answering for
Mankind's forlornest uses, thou canst pour
From thence into their ears. God's will devotes
Thine to such ends, and mine to wait on thine.
How, Dearest, wilt thou have me for most use?
A hope, to sing by gladly? ... or a fine
Sad memory, with thy songs to interfuse?
A shade, in which to sing ... of palm or pine?
A grave, on which to rest from singing? ... Choose.

XVIII

I never gave a lock of hair away
To a man, dearest, except this to thee,
Which now upon my fingers thoughtfully
I ring out to the full brown length and say
'Take it.' My day of youth went yesterday;
My hair no longer bounds to my foot's glee,
Nor plant I it from rose or myrtle-tree,
As girls do, any more. It only may
Now shade on two pale cheeks the mark of tears,
Taught drooping from the head that hangs aside
Through sorrow's trick. I thought the funeral-shears
Would take this first, but Love is justified, –
Take it thou, ... finding pure, from all those years,
The kiss my mother left here when she died.

XIX

The soul's Rialto hath its merchandise;
I barter curl for curl upon that mart,
And from my poet's forehead to my heart,
Receive this lock which outweighs argosies, –
As purply black, as erst, to Pindar's eyes
The dim purpureal tresses gloomed athwart
The nine white Muse-brows. For this counterpart, ...
The bay crown's shade, Belovèd, I surmise,
Still lingers on thy curl, it is so black!
Thus, with a fillet of smooth-kissing breath,
I tie the shadows safe from gliding back,
And lay the gift where nothing hindereth,
Here on my heart, as on thy brow, to lack
No natural heat till mine grows cold in death.

XX

Belovèd, my Belovèd, when I think
That thou wast in the world a year ago,
What time I sat alone here in the snow
And saw no footprint, heard the silence sink
No moment at thy voice, ... but, link by link,
Went counting all my chains, as if that so
They never could fall off at any blow
Struck by thy possible hand, ... why, thus I drink
Of life's great cup of wonder! Wonderful,
Never to feel thee thrill the day or night
With personal act or speech, – nor ever cull
Some prescience of thee with the blossoms white
Thou sawest growing! Atheists are as dull,
Who cannot guess God's presence out of sight.

XXI

Say over again, and yet once over again,
That thou dost love me. Though the word repeated
Should seem 'a cuckoo-song', as thou dost treat it.
Remember, never to the hill or plain,
Valley and wood, without her cuckoo-strain,
Comes the fresh Spring in all her green completed.
Belovèd, I, amid the darkness greeted
By a doubtful spirit-voice, in that doubt's pain
Cry ... 'Speak once more ... thou lovest!' Who can fear
Too many stars, though each in heaven shall roll –
Too many flowers, though each shall crown the year?
Say thou dost love me, love me, love me – toll
The silver iterance! – only minding, dear,
To love me also in silence, with thy soul.

XXII

When our two souls stand up erect and strong,
Face to face, silent, drawing nigh and nigher,
Until the lengthening wings break into fire
At either curvèd point, – what bitter wrong
Can the earth do to us, that we should not long
Be here contented? Think. In mounting higher,
The angels would press on us, and aspire
To drop some golden orb of perfect song
Into our deep, dear silence. Let us stay
Rather on earth, Belovèd, –where the unfit
Contrarious moods of men recoil away
And isolate pure spirits, and permit
A place to stand and love in for a day,
With darkness and the death-hour rounding it.

XXIII

Is it indeed so? If I lay here dead,
Wouldst thou miss any life in losing mine?
And would the sun for thee more coldly shine,
Because of grave-damps falling round my head?
I marvelled, my Belovèd, when I read
Thy thought so in the letter. I am thine –
But ... so much to thee? Can I pour thy wine
While my hands tremble? Then my soul, instead
Of dreams of death, resumes life's lower range.
Then, love me, Love! look on me ... breathe on me!
As brighter ladies do not count it strange,
For love, to give up acres and degree,
I yield the grave for thy sake, and exchange
My near sweet view of Heaven, for earth with thee!

XXIV

Let the world's sharpness like a clasping knife
Shut in upon itself and do no harm
In this close hand of Love, now soft and warm,
And let us hear no sound of human strife
After the click of the shutting. Life to life –
I lean upon thee, dear, without alarm,
And feel as safe as guarded by a charm
Against the stab of worldlings, who if rife
Are weak to injure. Very whitely still
The lilies of our lives may reassure
Their blossoms from their roots, accessible
Alone to heavenly dews that drop not fewer:
Growing straight, out of man's reach, on the hill.
God only, who made us rich, can make us poor.

XXV

A heavy heart, Belovèd, have I borne
From year to year until I saw thy face,
And sorrow after sorrow took the place
Of all those natural joys as lightly worn
As the stringed pearls ... each lifted in its turn
By a beating heart at dance-time. Hopes apace
Were changed to long despairs, till God's own grace
Could scarcely lift above the world forlorn
My heavy heart. Then thou didst bid me bring
And let it drop adown thy calmly great
Deep being! Fast it sinketh, as a thing
Which its own nature does precipitate,
While thine doth close above it, mediating
Betwixt the stars and the unaccomplished fate.

XXVI

I lived with visions for my company,
Instead of men and women, years ago,
And found them gentle mates, nor thought to know
A sweeter music than they played to me.
But soon their trailing purple was not free
Of this world's dust ... their lutes did silent grow,
And I myself grew faint and blind below
Their vanishing eyes. Then THOU didst come ... to be,
Belovèd, what they seemed. Their shining fronts,
Their songs, their splendours (better, yet the same,
As river-water hallowed into fonts),
Met in thee, and from out thee overcame
My soul with satisfaction of all wants –
Because God's gifts put man's best dreams to shame.

XXVII

My own Belovèd, who hast lifted me
From this drear flat of earth where I was thrown,
And, in betwixt the languid ringlets, blown
A life-breath, till the forehead hopefully
Shines out again, as all the angels see,
Before thy saving kiss! My own, my own,
Who camest to me when the world was gone,
And I who looked for only God, found thee!
I find thee; I am safe, and strong, and glad.
As one who stands in dewless asphodel,
Looks backward on the tedious time he had
In the upper life, – so I, with bosom-swell,
Make witness, here, between the good and bad,
That Love, as strong as Death, retrieves as well.

XXVIII

My letters! all dead paper, ... mute and white! –
And yet they seem alive and quivering
Against my tremulous hands which loose the string
And let them drop down on my knee tonight.
This said, ... he wished to have me in his sight
Once, as a friend: this fixed a day in spring
To come and touch my hand ... a simple thing,
Yet I wept for it! – this, ... the paper's light ...
Said, Dear, I love thee; and I sank and quailed
As if God's future thundered on my past.
This said, I am thine – and so its ink has paled
With lying at my heart that beat too fast.
And this ... O Love, thy words have ill availed,
If, what this said, I dared repeat at last!

XXIX

I think of thee! — my thoughts do twine and bud
About thee, as wild vines, about a tree,
Put out broad leaves, and soon there's nought to see
Except the straggling green which hides the wood.
Yet, O my palm-tree, be it understood
I will not have my thoughts instead of thee
Who art dearer, better! Rather instantly
Renew thy presence. As a strong tree should,
Rustle thy boughs and set thy trunk all bare,
And let these bands of greenery which insphere thee,
Drop heavily down, ... burst, shattered, everywhere!
Because, in this deep joy to see and hear thee
And breathe within thy shadow a new air,
I do not think of thee — I am too near thee.

XXX

I see thine image through my tears tonight,
And yet today I saw thee smiling. How
Refer the cause? — Belovèd, is it thou
Or I, who makes me sad? The acolyte
Amid the chanted joy and thankful rite,
May so fall flat, with pale insensate brow,
On the altar-stair. I hear thy voice and vow
Perplexed, uncertain, since thou art out of sight,
As he, in his swooning ears, the choir's amen.
Belovèd, dost thou love? or did I see all
The glory as I dreamed, and fainted when
Too vehement light dilated my ideal,
For my soul's eyes? Will that light come again,
As now these tears come ... falling hot and real?

XXXI

Thou comest! all is said without a word.
I sit beneath thy looks, as children do
In the noon-sun, with souls that tremble through
Their happy eyelids from an unaverred
Yet prodigal inward joy. Behold, I erred
In that last doubt! and yet I cannot rue
The sin most, but the occasion ... that we two
Should for a moment stand unministered
By a mutual presence. Ah, keep near and close,
Thou dove-like help! and when my fears would rise,
With thy broad heart serenely interpose.
Brood down with thy divine sufficiencies
These thoughts which tremble when bereft of those,
Like callow birds left desert to the skies.

XXXII

The first time that the sun rose on thine oath
To love me, I looked forward to the moon
To slacken all those bonds which seemed too soon
And quickly tied to make a lasting troth.
Quick-loving hearts, I thought, may quickly loathe;
And, looking on myself, I seemed not one
For such man's love! – more like an out-of-tune
Worn viol, a good singer would be wroth
To spoil his song with, and which, snatched in haste,
Is laid down at the first ill-sounding note.
I did not wrong myself so, but I placed
A wrong on thee. For perfect strains may float
'Neath master-hands, from instruments defaced, –
And great souls, at one stroke, may do and dote.

XXXIII

Yes, call me by my pet-name! let me hear
The name I used to run at, when a child,
From innocent play, and leave the cowslips piled,
To glance up in some face that proved me dear
With the look of its eyes. I miss the clear
Fond voices, which, being drawn and reconciled
Into the music of Heaven's undefiled,
Call me no longer. Silence on the bier,
While I call God ... call God! — So let thy mouth
Be heir to those who are now exanimate.
Gather the north flowers to complete the south,
And catch the early love up in the late.
Yes, call me by that name, — and I, in truth,
With the same heart, will answer and not wait.

XXXIV

With the same heart, I said, I'll answer thee
As those, when thou shalt call me by my name —
Lo, the vain promise! is the same, the same,
Perplexed and ruffled by life's strategy?
When called before, I told how hastily
I dropped my flowers or brake off from a game,
To run and answer with the smile that came
At play last moment, and went on with me
Through my obedience. When I answer now,
I drop a grave thought — break from solitude;
Yet still my heart goes to thee ... ponder how ...
Not as to a single good, but all my good!
Lay thy hand on it, best one, and allow
That no child's foot could run fast as this blood.

XXXV

If I leave all for thee, wilt thou exchange
And be all to me? Shall I never miss
Home-talk and blessing and the common kiss
That comes to each in turn, nor count it strange,
When I look up, to drop on a new range
Of walls and floors ... another home than this?
Nay, wilt thou fill that place by me which is
Filled by dead eyes too tender to know change?
That's hardest. If to conquer love, has tried,
To conquer grief, tries more ... as all things prove;
For grief indeed is love and grief beside.
Alas, I have grieved so I am hard to love.
Yet love me — wilt thou? Open thy heart wide,
And fold within, the wet wings of thy dove.

XXXVI

When we met first and loved, I did not build
Upon the event with marble. Could it mean
To last, a love set pendulous between
Sorrow and sorrow? Nay, I rather thrilled,
Distrusting every light that seemed to gild
The onward path, and feared to overlean
A finger even. And, though I have grown serene
And strong since then, I think that God has willed
A still renewable fear ... O love, O troth ...
Lest these enclaspèd hands should never hold,
This mutual kiss drop down between us both
As an unowned thing, once the lips being cold.
And Love, be false! if he, to keep one oath,
Must lose one joy, by his life's star foretold.

XXXVII

Pardon, oh, pardon, that my soul should make,
Of all that strong divineness which I know
For thine and thee, an image only so
Formed of the sand, and fit to shift and break.
It is that distant years which did not take
Thy sovranty, recoiling with a blow,
Have forced my swimming brain to undergo
Their doubt and dread, and blindly to forsake
Thy purity of likeness and distort
Thy worthiest love to a worthless counterfeit.
As if a shipwrecked Pagan, safe in port,
His guardian sea-god to commemorate,
Should set a sculptured porpoise, gills a-snort
And vibrant tail, within the temple-gate.

XXXVIII

First time he kissed me, he but only kissed
The fingers of this hand wherewith I write;
And ever since, it grew more clean and white, ...
Slow to world-greetings ... quick with its 'Oh, list,'
When the angels speak. A ring of amethyst
I could not wear here, plainer to my sight,
Than that first kiss. The second passed in height
The first, and sought the forehead, and half missed,
Half falling on the hair. O beyond meed!
That was the chrism of love, which love's own crown,
With sanctifying sweetness, did precede.
The third upon my lips was folded down
In perfect, purple state; since when, indeed,
I have been proud and said, 'My love, my own.'

XXXIX

Because thou hast the power and own'st the grace
To look through and behind this mask of me
(Against which years have beat thus blanchingly
With their rains) and behold my soul's true face,
The dim and weary witness of life's race! —
Because thou hast the faith and love to see,
Through that same soul's distracting lethargy,
The patient angel waiting for a place
In the new heavens! because nor sin nor woe,
Nor God's infliction, nor death's neighbourhood,
Nor all which others viewing, turn to go, …
Nor all which makes me tired of all, self-viewed, …
Nothing repels thee, … dearest, teach me so
To pour out gratitude, as thou dost, good.

XL

Oh, yes! they love through all this world of ours!
I will not gainsay love, called love forsooth.
I have heard love talked in my early youth,
And since, not so long back but that the flowers
Then gathered, smell still. Mussulmans and Giaours
Throw kerchiefs at a smile, and have no ruth
For any weeping. Polypheme's white tooth
Slips on the nut, if, after frequent showers,
The shell is over-smooth, – and not so much
Will turn the thing called love, aside to hate,
Or else to oblivion. But thou art not such
A lover, my Belovèd! thou canst wait
Through sorrow and sickness, to bring souls to touch,
And think it soon when others cry 'Too late.'

XLI

I thank all who have loved me in their hearts,
With thanks and love from mine. Deep thanks to all
Who paused a little near the prison-wall,
To hear my music in its louder parts,
Ere they went onward, each one to the mart's
Or temple's occupation, beyond call.
But thou, who, in my voice's sink and fall,
When the sob took it, thy divinest Art's
Own instrument didst drop down at thy foot,
To harken what I said between my tears, . . .
Instruct me how to thank thee! – Oh, to shoot
My soul's full meaning into future years,
That they should lend it utterance, and salute
Love that endures, from Life that disappears!

XLII

'My future will not copy fair my past – '
I wrote that once; and thinking at my side
My ministering life-angel justified
The word by his appealing look upcast
To the white throne of God, I turned at last,
And there, instead, saw thee, not unallied
To angels in thy soul! Then I, long tried
By natural ills, received the comfort fast,
While budding, at thy sight, my pilgrim's staff
Gave out green leaves with morning dews impearled.
I seek no copy now of life's first half:
Leave here the pages with long musing curled,
And write me new my future's epigraph,
New angel mine, unhoped for in the world!

XLIII

How do I love thee? Let me count the ways.
I love thee to the depth and breadth and height
My soul can reach, when feeling out of sight
For the ends of Being and ideal Grace.
I love thee to the level of every day's
Most quiet need, by sun and candlelight.
I love thee freely, as men strive for Right;
I love thee purely, as they turn from Praise.
I love thee with the passion put to use
In my old griefs, and with my childhood's faith.
I love thee with a love I seemed to lose
With my lost saints, – I love thee with the breath,
Smiles, tears, of all my life! – and, if God choose,
I shall but love thee better after death.

XLIV

Belovèd, thou hast brought me many flowers
Plucked in the garden, all the summer through
And winter, and it seemed as if they grew
In this close room, nor missed the sun and showers.
So, in the like name of that love of ours,
Take back these thoughts which here unfolded too,
And which on warm and cold days I withdrew
From my heart's ground. Indeed, those beds and bowers
Be overgrown with bitter weeds and rue,
And wait thy weeding; yet here's eglantine,
Here's ivy! – take them, as I used to do
Thy flowers, and keep them where they shall not pine.
Instruct thine eyes to keep their colours true,
And tell thy soul, their roots are left in mine.

The Runaway Slave at Pilgrim's Point

I stand on the mark beside the shore
   Of the first white pilgrim's bended knee;
Where exile turned to ancestor,
   And God was thanked for liberty.
I have run through the night, my skin is as dark,
I bend my knee down on this mark ...
   I look on the sky and the sea.

O pilgrim-souls, I speak to you!
   I see you come out proud and slow
From the land of the spirits pale as dew,
   And round me and round me ye go!
O pilgrims, I have gasped and run
All night long from the whips of one
   Who in your names works sin and woe.

And thus I thought that I would come
   And kneel here where I knelt before,
And feel your souls around me hum
   In undertone to the ocean's roar;
And lift my black face, my black hand,
Here, in your names, to curse this land
   Ye blessed in freedom's evermore.

I am black, I am black!
   And yet God made me, they say;
But if He did so, smiling back
   He must have cast His work away
Under the feet of His white creatures,
With a look of scorn, – that the dusky features
   Might be trodden again to clay.

And yet He has made dark things
  To be glad and merry as light:
There's a little dark bird sits and sings;
  There's a dark stream ripples out of sight;
And the dark frogs chant in the safe morass,
And the sweetest stars are made to pass
  O'er the face of the darkest night.

But *we* who are dark, we are dark!
  Ah, God, we have no stars!
About our souls in care and cark
  Our blackness shuts like prison bars;
The poor souls crouch so far behind
That never a comfort can they find
  By reaching through the prison-bars.

Indeed, we live beneath the sky,
  That great smooth Hand of God stretched out
On all His children fatherly,
  To save them from the fear and doubt
Which would be, if, from this low place,
All opened straight up to His face
  Into the grand eternity.

And still God's sunshine and His frost,
  They make us hot, they make us cold,
As if we were not black and lost:
  And the beasts and birds, in wood and fold,
Do fear and take us for very men!
Could the whip-poor-will or the cat of the glen
  Look into my eyes and be bold?

I am black, I am black! —
  But, once, I laughed in girlish glee,
For one of my colour stood in the track
  Where the drivers drove, and looked at me,
And tender and full was the look he gave —
Could a slave look so at another slave? —
  I look at the sky and the sea.

And from that hour our spirits grew
  As free as if unsold, unbought:
Oh, strong enough, since we were two,
  To conquer the world, we thought!
The drivers drove us day by day:
We did not mind, we went one way,
  And no better a liberty sought.

In the sunny ground between the canes,
  He said 'I love you' as he passed:
When the shingle-roof rang sharp with the rains,
  I heard how he vowed it fast;
While others shook he smiled in the hut,
As he carved me a bowl of the cocoa-nut
  Through the roar of the hurricanes.

I sang his name instead of a song,
  Over and over I sang his name —
Upward and downward I drew it along
  My various notes, — the same, the same!
I sang it low, that the slave-girls near
Might never guess from aught they could hear,
  It was only a name — a name.

I look on the sky and the sea.
  We were two to love, and two to pray, —
Yes, two, O God, who cried to Thee,
  Though nothing didst Thou say.
Coldly Thou sat'st behind the sun!
And now I cry who am but one,
  Thou wilt not speak today. —

We were black, we were black,
  We had no claim to love and bliss,
What marvel, if each went to wrack?
  They wrung my cold hands out of his, —
They dragged him ... where? ... I crawled to touch
His blood's mark in the dust! ... not much,
  Ye pilgrim-souls, ... though plain as this!

Wrong, followed by a deeper wrong!
  Mere grief's too good for such as I;
So the white men brought the shame ere long
  To strangle the sob of my agony.
They would not leave me for my dull
Wet eyes! — it was too merciful
  To let me weep pure tears and die.

I am black, I am black!
  I wore a child upon my breast ...
An amulet that hung too slack,
  And, in my unrest, could not rest.
Thus we went moaning, child and mother,
One to another, one to another,
  Until all ended for the best:

For hark! I will tell you low ... low ...
  I am black, you see, –
And the babe who lay on my bosom so,
  Was far too white ... too white for me;
As white as the ladies who scorned to pray
Beside me at church but yesterday,
  Though my tears had washed a place for my knee.

My own, own child! I could not bear
  To look in his face, it was so white;
I covered him up with a kerchief there;
  I covered his face in close and tight:
And he moaned and struggled, as well might be,
For the white child wanted his liberty –
  Ha, ha! he wanted his master-right.

He moaned and beat with his head and feet,
  His little feet that never grew –
He struck them out, as it was meet,
  Against my heart to break it through.
I might have sung and made him mild –
But I dared not sing to the white-faced child
  The only song I knew.

I pulled the kerchief very close:
  He could not see the sun, I swear,
More, then, alive, than now he does
  From between the roots of the mango ... where?
... I know where. Close! A child and mother
Do wrong to look at one another
  When one is black and one is fair.

Why, in that single glance I had
   Of my child's face, ... I tell you all,
I saw a look that made me mad!
   The master's look, that used to fall
On my soul like his lash ... or worse! —
And so, to save it from my curse,
   I twisted it round in my shawl.

And he moaned and trembled from foot to head,
   He shivered from head to foot;
Till, after a time, he lay instead
   Too suddenly still and mute.
I felt, beside, a stiffening cold, ...
I dared to lift up just a fold ...
   As in lifting a leaf of the mango-fruit.

But my fruit ... ha, ha! — there, had been
   (I laugh to think on't at this hour!)
Your fine white angels, (who have seen
   Nearest the secret of God's power)
And plucked my fruit to make them wine,
And sucked the soul of that child of mine,
   As the humming-bird sucks the soul of the flower.

Ha, ha, the trick of the angels white!
   They freed the white child's spirit so.
I said not a word, but, day and night,
   I carried the body to and fro,
And it lay on my heart like a stone ... as chill.
   — The sun may shine out as much as he will:
   I am cold, though it happened a month ago.

From the white man's house, and the black man's hut,
  I carried the little body on;
The forest's arms did round us shut,
  And silence through the trees did run.
They asked no question as I went, —
They stood too high for astonishment, —
  They could see God sit on His throne.

My little body, kerchiefed fast,
  I bore it on through the forest … on;
And when I felt it was tired at last,
  I scooped a hole beneath the moon.
Through the forest-tops the angels far,
With a white sharp finger from every star,
  Did point and mock at what was done.

Yet when it was all done aright, …
  Earth, 'twixt me and my baby, strewed, …
All, changed to black earth, … nothing white …
  A dark child in the dark! — ensued
Some comfort, and my heart grew young;
I sat down smiling there and sung
  The song I learnt in my maidenhood.

And thus we two were reconciled,
  The white child and black mother, thus;
For, as I sang it soft and wild,
  The same song, more melodious,
Rose from the grave whereon I sat:
It was the dead child singing that,
  To join the souls of both of us.

I look on the sea and the sky!
  Where the pilgrims' ships first anchored lay
The free sun rideth gloriously,
  But the pilgrim-ghosts have slid away
Through the earliest streaks of the morn:
My face is black, but it glares with a scorn
  Which they dare not meet by day.

Ah! – in their 'stead, their hunter sons!
  Ah, ah! they are on me – they hunt in a ring –
Keep off! I brave you all at once –
  I throw off your eyes like snakes that sting!
You have killed the black eagle at nest, I think:
Did you never stand still in your triumph, and shrink
  From the stroke of her wounded wing?

(Man, drop that stone you dared to lift! –)
  I wish you, who stand there five abreast,
Each, for his own wife's joy and gift,
  A little corpse as safely at rest
As mine in the mangos! Yes, but she
May keep live babies on her knee,
  And sing the song she likes best.

I am not mad: I am black.
  I see you staring in my face –
I know you staring, shrinking back,
  Ye are born of the Washington-race,
And this land is the free America,
And this mark on my wrist ... (I prove what I say)
  Ropes tied me up here to the flogging-place.

You think I shrieked then? Not a sound!
   I hung, as a gourd hangs in the sun;
I only cursed them all around
   As softly as I might have done
My very own child. – From these sands
Up to the mountains, lift your hands,
   O slaves, and end what I begun!

Whips, curses; these must answer those!
   For in this UNION, you have set
Two kinds of men in adverse rows,
   Each loathing each: and all forget
The seven wounds in Christ's body fair,
While HE sees gaping everywhere
   Our countless wounds that pay no debt.

Our wounds are different. Your white men
   Are, after all, not gods indeed,
Nor able to make Christs again
   Do good with bleeding. *We* who bleed
(Stand off!) we help not in our loss!
We are too heavy for our cross,
   And fall and crush you and your seed.

I fall, I swoon! I look at the sky:
   The clouds are breaking on my brain:
I am floated along, as if I should die
   Of liberty's exquisite pain.
In the name of the white child waiting for me
In the death-dark where we may kiss and agree,
White men, I leave you all curse-free
   In my broken heart's disdain!

A Flower in a Letter

My lonely chamber next the sea
Is full of many flowers set free
   By summer's earliest duty:
Dear friends upon the garden-walk
Might stop amid their fondest talk
   To pull the least in beauty.

A thousand flowers – each seeming one
That learnt by gazing on the sun
   To counterfeit his shining;
Within whose leaves the holy dew
That falls from heaven has won anew
   A glory, in declining.

Red roses, used to praises long,
Contented with the poet's song,
   The nightingale's being over;
And lilies white, prepared to touch
The whitest thought, nor soil it much,
   Of dreamer turned to lover.

Deep violets, you liken to
The kindest eyes that look on you,
   Without a thought disloyal;
And cactuses a queen might don,
If weary of a golden crown,
   And still appear as royal.

Pansies for ladies all – (wis
That none who wear such brooches, miss

A jewel in the mirror);
And tulips, children love to stretch
Their fingers down, to feel in each
   Its beauty's secret nearer.

Love's language may be talked with these;
To work out choicest sentences
   No blossoms can be meeter;
And, such being used in Eastern bowers,
Young maids may wonder if the flowers
   Or meanings be the sweeter.

And such being strewn before a bride,
Her little foot may turn aside,
   Their longer bloom decreeing,
Unless some voice's whispered sound
Should make her gaze upon the ground
   Too earnestly – for seeing.

And such being scattered on a grave,
Whoever mourneth there, may have
   A type which seemeth worthy
Of that fair body hid below,
Which bloomed on earth a time ago,
   Then perished as the earthy.

And such being wreathed for worldly feast,
Across the brimming cup some guest
   Their rainbow colours viewing,
May feel them, with a silent start,
The covenant, his childish heart
   With nature made – renewing.

No flowers our gardened England hath
To match with these, in bloom and breath,
  Which from the world are hiding,
In sunny Devon moist with rills, —
A nunnery of cloistered hills,
  The elements presiding.

By Loddon's stream the flowers are fair
That meet one gifted lady's care
  With prodigal rewarding
(For Beauty is too used to run
To Mitford's bower — to want the sun
  To light her through the garden).

But, here, all summers are comprised —
The nightly frosts shrink exorcised
  Before the priestly moonshine;
And every wind with stolèd feet,
In wandering down the alleys sweet,
  Steps lightly on the sunshine.

And (having promised Harpocrate
Among the nodding roses that
  No harm shall touch his daughters)
Gives quite away the rushing sound,
He dares not use upon such ground,
  To ever-trickling waters.

Yet, sun and wind! what can ye do
But make the leaves more brightly show
  In posies newly gathered?
I look away from all your best,

To one poor flower unlike the rest,
  A little flower half-withered.

I do not think it ever was
A pretty flower, — to make the grass
  Look greener where it reddened;
And now it seems ashamed to be
Alone, in all this company,
  Of aspect shrunk and saddened.

A chamber-window was the spot
It grew in, from a garden-pot,
  Among the city shadows.
If any, tending it, might seem
To smile, 'twas only in a dream
  Of nature in the meadows.

How coldly on its head did fall
The sunshine, from the city wall
  In pale refraction driven!
How sadly, plashed upon its leaves,
The raindrops, losing in the eaves
  The first sweet news of heaven!

And those who planted, gathered it
In gamesome or in loving fit,
  And sent it as a token
Of what their city pleasures be, —
For one, in Devon by the sea
  And garden-blooms, to look on.

But SHE, for whom the jest was meant,
With a grave passion innocent
  Receiving what was given, —
Oh, if her face she turnèd then,
Let none say 'twas to gaze again
  Upon the flowers of Devon!

Because, whatever virtue dwells
In genial skies, warm oracles
  For gardens brightly springing, —
The flower which grew beneath your eyes,
Belovèd friends, to mine supplies
  A beauty worthier singing!

A Sabbath Morning at Sea

The ship went on with solemn face;
  To meet the darkness on the deep,
    The solemn ship went onward.
I bowed down weary in the place,
  For parting tears and present sleep
    Had weighed mine eyelids downward.

Thick sleep which shut all dreams from me,
  And kept my inner self apart
    And quiet from emotion,
Then brake away and left me free,
  Made conscious of a human heart
    Betwixt the heaven and ocean.

The new sight, the new wondrous sight!
  The waters round me, turbulent, –
    The skies impassive o'er me,
Calm, in a moonless, sunless light,
  Half glorified by that intent
    Of holding the day-glory!

Two pale thin clouds did stand upon
  The meeting line of sea and sky,
    With aspect still and mystic.
I think they did foresee the sun,
  And rested on their prophecy
    In quietude majestic,

Then flushed to radiance where they stood,
  Like statues by the open tomb

Of shining saints half risen. —
The sun! — he came up to be viewed,
  And sky and sea made mighty room
    To inaugurate the vision.

I oft had seen the dawnlight run,
  As red wine through the hills, and break
    Through many a mist's inurning;
But, here, no earth profaned the sun!
  Heaven, ocean, did alone partake
    The sacrament of morning.

Away with thoughts fantastical!
  I would be humble to my worth,
    Self-guarded as self-doubted:
Though here no earthly shadows fall,
  I, joying, grieving without earth,
    May desecrate without it.

God's sabbath morning sweeps the waves;
  I would not praise the pageant high,
    Yet miss the dedicature.
I, carried toward the sunless graves
  By force of natural things, — should I
    Exult in only nature?

And could I bear to sit alone
  'Mid nature's fixed benignities,
    While my warm pulse was moving?
Too dark thou art, O glittering sun,
  Too strait ye are, capacious seas,
    To satisfy the loving!

It seems a better lot than so,
   To sit with friends beneath the beech,
     And feel them dear and dearer;
Or follow children as they go
   In pretty pairs, with softened speech,
     As the church-bells ring nearer.

Love me, sweet friends, this sabbath day!
   The sea sings round me while ye roll
     Afar the hymn unaltered,
And kneel, where once I knelt to pray,
   And bless me deeper in the soul,
     Because the voice has faltered.

And though this sabbath comes to me
   Without the stolèd minister
     Or chanting congregation,
God's Spirit brings communion, HE
   Who brooded soft on waters drear,
     Creator on creation.

Himself, I think, shall draw me higher,
   Where keep the saints with harp and song
     An endless sabbath morning,
And on that sea commixed with fire
   Oft drop their eyelids, raised too long
     To the full Godhead's burning.

A Dead Rose

O Rose! who dares to name thee?
No longer roseate now, nor soft, nor sweet,
But pale, and hard, and dry, as stubble-wheat, –
    Kept seven years in a drawer – thy titles shame thee.

    The breeze that used to blow thee
Between the hedgerow thorns, and take away
An odour up the lane to last all day, –
    If breathing now, – unsweetened would forego thee.

    The sun that used to smite thee,
And mix his glory in thy gorgeous urn
Till beam appeared to bloom, and flower to burn, –
    If shining now, – with not a hue would light thee.

    The dew that used to wet thee,
And, white first, grow incarnadined, because
It lay upon thee where the crimson was, –
    If dropping now, – would darken, where it met thee.

    The fly that 'it upon thee,
To stretch the tendrils of its tiny feet,
Along thy leaf's pure edges, after heat,—
    If 'ighting now, – would coldly overrun thee.

    The bee that once did suck thee,
And build thy perfumed ambers up his hive,
And swoon in thee for joy, till scarce alive, –
    If passing now, – would blindly overlook thee.

The heart doth recognise thee,
Alone, alone! The heart doth smell thee sweet,
Doth view thee fair, doth judge thee most complete,
  Perceiving all those changes that disguise thee.

  Yes, and the heart doth owe thee
More love, dead rose, than to such roses bold
Which Julia wears at dances, smiling cold! –
  Lie still upon this heart – which breaks below thee!

A Child's Thought of God

They say that God lives very high:
   But if you look above the pines
You cannot see our God; and why?

And if you dig down in the mines
   You never see Him in the gold;
Though, from Him, all that's glory shines.

God is so good, He wears a fold
   Of heaven and earth across His face –
Like secrets kept, for love, untold.

But still I feel that His embrace
   Slides down by thrills, through all things made,
Through sight and sound of every place.

As if my tender mother laid
   On my shut lids her kisses' pressure,
Half-waking me at night and said
   'Who kissed you through the dark, dear guesser?'

Life and Love

Fast this Life of mine was dying,
   Blind already and calm as death,
Snowflakes on her bosom lying
   Scarcely heaving with her breath.

Love came by, and having known her
   In a dream of fabled lands,
Gently stooped, and laid upon her
   Mystic chrism of holy hands;

Drew his smile across her folded
   Eyelids, as the swallow dips:
Breathed as finely as the cold did,
   Through the locking of her lips.

So, when Life looked upward, being
   Warmed and breathed on from above,
What sight could she have for seeing,
   Evermore ... but only LOVE?

Love

We cannot live, except thus mutually
We alternate, aware or unaware,
The reflex act of life; and when we bear
Our virtue outward most impulsively,
Most full of invocation, and to be
Most instantly compellant, certes, there
We live most life, whoever breathes most air,
And counts his dying years by sun and sea.
But when a soul, by choice and conscience, doth
Throw out her full force on another soul,
The conscience and the concentration both
Make mere life, Love. For Life in perfect whole
And aim consummated, is Love in sooth,
As nature's magnet-heat rounds pole with pole.

Human Life's Mystery

We sow the glebe, we reap the corn,
  We build the house where we may rest,
And then, at moments, suddenly
We look up to the great wide sky,
Inquiring wherefore we were born...
  For earnest, or for jest?

The senses folding thick and dark
  About the stifled soul within,
We guess diviner things beyond,
And yearn to them with yearning fond;
We strike out blindly to a mark
  Believed in, but not seen.

We vibrate to the pant and thrill
  Wherewith Eternity has curled
In serpent-twine about God's seat;
While, freshening upward to His feet,
In gradual growth His full-leaved will
  Expands from world to world.

And, in the tumult and excess
  Of act and passion under sun,
We sometimes hear – oh, soft and far,
As silver star did touch with star,
The kiss of Peace and Righteousness
  Through all things that are done.

God keeps His holy mysteries
  Just on the outside of man's dream.

In diapason slow, we think
To hear their pinions rise and sink,
While they float pure beneath His eyes,
  Like swans adown a stream.

Abstractions, are they, from the forms
  Of His great beauty? – exaltations
From His great glory? – strong previsions
Of what we shall be? – intuitions
Of what we are – in calms and storms,
  Beyond our peace and passions?

Things nameless! which, in passing so,
  Do stroke us with a subtle grace.
We say, 'Who passes?' – they are dumb.
We cannot see them go or come:
Their touches fall soft – cold – as snow
  Upon a blind man's face.

Yet, touching so, they draw above
  Our common thoughts to Heaven's unknown;
Our daily joy and pain, advance
To a divine significance, –
Our human love – O mortal love,
  That light is not its own!

And sometimes horror chills our blood
  To be so near such mystic Things,
And we wrap round us for defence,
Our purple manners, moods of sense –
As angels, from the face of God,
  Stand hidden in their wings.

And, sometimes, through life's heavy swound
  We grope for them! – with strangled breath
We stretch our hands abroad and try
To reach them in our agony, –
And widen, so, the broad life-wound
  Which soon is large enough for death.

A Man's Requirements

Love me, sweet, with all thou art,
  Feeling, thinking, seeing, —
Love me in the lightest part,
  Love me in full being.

Love me with thine open youth
  In its frank surrender;
With the vowing of thy mouth,
  With its silence tender.

Love me with thine azure eyes,
  Made for earnest grantings!
Taking colour from the skies,
  Can Heaven's truth be wanting?

Love me with their lids, that fall
  Snow-like at first meeting;
Love me with thine heart, that all
  The neighbours then see beating.

Love me with thine hand stretched out
  Freely — open-minded;
Love me with thy loitering foot, —
  Hearing one behind it.

Love me with thy voice, that turns
  Sudden faint above me;
Love me with thy blush that burns
  When I murmur, *Love me!*

Love me with thy thinking soul —
  Break it to love-sighing;
Love me with thy thoughts that roll
  On through living — dying.

Love me in thy gorgeous airs,
  When the world has crowned thee!
Love me, kneeling at thy prayers,
  With the angels round thee.

Love me pure, as musers do,
  Up the woodlands shady;
Love me gaily, fast, and true,
  As a winsome lady.

Through all hopes that keep us brave,
  Further off or nigher,
Love me for the house and grave, —
  And for something higher.

Thus, if thou wilt prove me, dear,
  Woman's love no fable.
I will love thee — half a year —
  As a man is able.

I had a little chamber in the house
(from *Aurora Leigh*)

I had a little chamber in the house,
As green as any privet-hedge a bird
Might choose to build in, though the nest itself
Could show but dead brown sticks and straws; the walls
Were green, the carpet was pure green, the straight
Small bed was curtained greenly, and the folds
Hung green about the window, which let in
The outdoor world with all its greenery.
You could not push your head out and escape
A dash of dawn-dew from the honeysuckle,
But so you were baptised into the grace
And privilege of seeing...
                                        First, the lime
(I had enough there, of the lime, be sure, –
My morning-dream was often hummed away
By the bees in it), past the lime, the lawn,
Which, after sweeping broadly round the house,
Went trickling through the shrubberies in a stream
Of tender turf, and wore and lost itself
Among the acacias, over which you saw
The irregular line of elms by the deep lane
Which stopped the grounds and dammed the overflow
Of arbutus and laurel. Out of sight
The lane was; sunk so deep, no foreign tramp
Nor drover of wild ponies out of Wales
Could guess if lady's hall or tenant's lodge
Dispensed such odours, – though his stick well-crooked
Might reach the lowest trail of blossoming briar
Which dipped upon the wall. Behind the elms,

And through their tops, you saw the folded hills
Striped up and down with hedges (burly oaks
Projecting from the line to show themselves),
Through which my cousin Romney's chimneys smoked
As still as when a silent month in frost
Breathes, showing where the woodlands hid Leigh Hall;
While, far above, a jut of table-land,
A promontory without water, stretched, –
You could not catch it if the days were thick,
Or took it for a cloud; but, otherwise,
The vigorous sun would catch it up at eve
And use it for an anvil till he had filled
The shelves of heaven with burning thunderbolts,
Protesting against night and darkness: – then,
When all his setting trouble was resolved
To a trance of passive glory, you might see
In apparition on the golden sky
(Alas, my Giotto's background!) the sheep run
Along the fine clear outline, small as mice
That run along a witch's scarlet thread.

A Denial

We have met late — it is too late to meet,
  O friend, not more than friend!
Death's forecome shroud is tangled round my feet,
And if I step or stir, I touch the end.
  In this last jeopardy
Can I approach thee, I, who cannot move?
How shall I answer thy request for love?
  Look in my face and see.

I love thee not, I dare not love thee! go
  In silence; drop my hand.
If thou seek roses, seek them where they blow
In garden-alleys, not in desert-sand.
  Can life and death agree,
That thou shouldst stoop thy song to my complaint?
I cannot love thee. If the word is faint,
  Look in my face and see.

I might have loved thee in some former days.
  Oh, then, my spirits had leapt
As now they sink, at hearing thy love-praise.
Before these faded cheeks were overwept,
  Had this been asked of me,
To love thee with my whole strong heart and head, —
I should have said still ... yes, but *smiled* and said,
  'Look in my face and see!'

But now ... God sees me, God, who took my heart
  And drowned it in life's surge.
In all your wide warm earth I have no part —

A light song overcomes me like a dirge.
  Could Love's great harmony
The saints keep step to when their bonds are loose,
Not weigh me down? am I a wife to choose?
  Look in my face and see.

While I behold, as plain as one who dreams,
  Some woman of full worth,
Whose voice, as cadenced as a silver stream's,
Shall prove the fountain-soul which sends it forth;
  One younger, more thought-free
And fair and gay, than I, thou must forget,
With brighter eyes than these ... which are not wet ...
  Look in my face and see!

So farewell thou, whom I have known too late
  To let thee come so near.
Be counted happy while men call thee great,
And one belovèd woman feels thee dear! –
  Not I! – that cannot be.
I am lost, I am changed, – I must go farther, where
The change shall take me worse, and no one dare
  Look in my face to see.

Meantime I bless thee. By these thoughts of mine
  I bless thee from all such!
I bless thy lamp to oil, thy cup to wine,
Thy hearth to joy, thy hand to an equal touch
  Of loyal troth. For me,
I love thee not, I love thee not! – away!
Here's no more courage in my soul to say
  'Look in my face and see.'

Italy and the World

Florence, Bologna, Parma, Modena.
  When you named them a year ago,
So many graves reserved by God, in a
  Day of Judgment, you seemed to know,
To open and let out the resurrection.

And meantime (you made your reflection
  If you were English), was nought to be done
But sorting sables, in predilection
  For all those martyrs dead and gone,
Till the new earth and heaven made ready?

And if your politics were not heady,
Violent, ... 'Good,' you added, 'good
In all things! Mourn on sure and steady.
Churchyard thistles are wholesome food
For our European wandering asses.

'The date of the resurrection passes
  Human foreknowledge: men unborn
Will gain by it (even in the lower classes),
  But none of these. It is not the morn
Because the cock of France is crowing.

'Cocks crow at midnight, seldom knowing
  Starlight from dawn-light: 'tis a mad
Poor creature.' Here you paused, and growing
  Scornful, ... suddenly, let us add,
The trumpet sounded, the graves were open.

Life and life and life! agrope in
  The dusk of death, warm hands, stretched out
For swords, proved more life still to hope in,
  Beyond and behind. Arise with a shout,
Nation of Italy, slain and buried!

Hill to hill and turret to turret
  Flashing the tricolor, – newly created
Beautiful Italy, calm, unhurried,
  Rise heroic and renovated,
Rise to the final restitution.

Rise; prefigure the grand solution
  Of earth's municipal, insular schisms, –
Statesmen draping self-love's conclusion
  In cheap vernacular patriotisms,
Unable to give up Judæa for Jesus.

Bring us the higher example; release us
  Into the larger coming time:
And into Christ's broad garment piece us
  Rags of virtue as poor as crime,
National selfishness, civic vaunting.

No more Jew nor Greek then, – taunting
  Nor taunted; – no more England nor France!
But one confederate brotherhood planting
  One flag only, to mark the advance,
Onward and upward, of all humanity.

For civilisation perfected
  Is fully developed Christianity.

'Measure the frontier,' shall it be said,
  'Count the ships,' in national vanity?
− Count the nation's heart-beats sooner.

For, though behind by a cannon or schooner,
  That nation still is predominant,
Whose pulse beats quickest in zeal to
  oppugn or
  Succour another, in wrong or want,
Passing the frontier in love and abhorrence.

Modena, Parma, Bologna, Florence,
  Open us out the wider way!
Dwarf in that chapel of old Saint Lawrence
  Your Michel Angelo's giant Day,
With the grandeur of this Day breaking o'er us!

Ye who, restrained as an ancient chorus,
  Mute while the coryphæus spake,
Hush your separate voices before us,
  Sink your separate lives for the sake
Of one sole Italy's living for ever!

Givers of coat and cloak too, − never
  Grudging that purple of yours at the best, −
By your heroic will and endeavour
  Each sublimely dispossessed,
That all may inherit what each surrenders!

Earth shall bless you, O noble emenders
  On egotist nations! Ye shall lead
The plough of the world, and sow new splendours

Into the furrow of things for seed, –
Ever the richer for what ye have given.

Lead us and teach us, till earth and heaven
   Grow larger around us and higher above.
Our sacrament-bread has a bitter leaven;
   We bait our traps with the name of love,
Till hate itself has a kinder meaning.

Oh, this world: this cheating and screening
   Of cheats! this conscience for candle-wicks,
Not beacon-fires! this overweening
   Of underhand diplomatical tricks,
Dared for the country while scorned for the
   counter!

Oh, this envy of those who mount here,
   And oh, this malice to make them trip!
Rather quenching the fire there, drying the fount
   here,
   To frozen body and thirsty lip,
Than leave to a neighbour their ministration.

I cry aloud in my poet-passion,
   Viewing my England o'er Alp and sea.
I loved her more in her ancient fashion:
   She carries her rifles too thick for me,
Who spares them so in the cause of a brother.

Suspicion, panic? end this pother.
   The sword, kept sheathless at peace-time, rusts.
None fears for himself while he feels for another:

The brave man either fights or trusts,
And wears no mail in his private chamber.

Beautiful Italy! golden amber
  Warm with the kisses of lover and traitor!
Thou who hast drawn us on to remember,
  Draw us to hope now: let us be greater
By this new future than that old story.

Till truer glory replaces all glory,
  As the torch grows blind at the dawn of day;
And the nations, rising up, their sorry
  And foolish sins shall put away,
As children their toys when the teacher enters.

Till Love's one centre devour these centres
  Of many self-loves; and the patriot's trick
To better his land by egotist ventures,
  Defamed from a virtue, shall make men sick,
As the scalp at the belt of some red hero.

For certain virtues have dropped to zero,
  Left by the sun on the mountain's dewy side;
Churchman's charities, tender as Nero,
  Indian suttee, heathen suicide,
Service to rights divine, proved hollow:

And Heptarchy patriotisms must follow.
  – National voices, distinct yet dependent,
Ensphering each other, as swallow does swallow,
  With circles still widening and ever ascendant,
In multiform life to united progression, –

These shall remain. And when, in the session
  Of nations, the separate language is heard,
Each shall aspire, in sublime indiscretion,
  To help with a thought or exalt with a word
Less her own than her rival's honour.

Each Christian nation shall take upon her
  The law of the Christian man in vast:
The crown of the getter shall fall to the donor,
  And last shall be first while first shall be last,
And to love best shall still be, to reign unsurpassed.

A Curse for a Nation

Prologue

I heard an angel speak last night,
And he said 'Write!
Write a Nation's curse for me,
And send it over the Western Sea.'

I faltered, taking up the word:
'Not so, my lord!
If curses must be, choose another
To send thy curse against my brother.

'For I am bound by gratitude,
By love and blood,
To brothers of mine across the sea,
Who stretch out kindly hands to me.'

'Therefore,' the voice said, 'shalt thou write
My curse to-night.
From the summits of love a curse is driven,
As lightning is from the tops of heaven.'

'Not so,' I answered. 'Evermore
My heart is sore
For my own land's sins: for little feet
Of children bleeding along the street:

'For parked-up honours that gainsay
The right of way:
For almsgiving through a door that is
Not open enough for two friends to kiss:

'For love of freedom which abates
Beyond the Straits:
For patriot virtue starved to vice on
Self-praise, self-interest, and suspicion:

'For an oligarchic parliament,
And bribes well-meant.
What curse to another land assign,
When heavy-souled for the sins of mine?'

'Therefore,' the voice said, 'shalt thou write
My curse to-night.
Because thou hast strength to see and hate
A foul thing done within thy gate.'

'Not so,' I answered once again.
'To curse, choose men.
For I, a woman, have only known
How the heart melts and the tears run down.'

'Therefore,' the voice said, 'shalt thou write
My curse to-night.
Some women weep and curse, I say
(And no one marvels), night and day.

'And thou shalt take their part to-night,
Weep and write.
A curse from the depths of womanhood
Is very salt, and bitter, and good.'

So thus I wrote, and mourned indeed,
What all may read.

And thus, as was enjoined on me,
I send it over the Western Sea.

The Curse

I

Because ye have broken your own chain
With the strain
Of brave men climbing a Nation's height,
Yet thence bear down with brand and thong
On souls of others, – for this wrong
This is the curse. Write.

Because yourselves are standing straight
In the state
Of Freedom's foremost acolyte,
Yet keep calm footing all the time
On writhing bond-slaves, – for this crime
This is the curse. Write.

Because ye prosper in God's name,
With a claim
To honour in the old world's sight,
Yet do the fiend's work perfectly
In strangling martyrs, – for this lie
This is the curse. Write.

II

Ye shall watch while kings conspire
Round the people's smouldering fire,
And, warm for your part,
Shall never dare – O shame!
To utter the thought into flame

Which burns at your heart.
This is the curse. Write.

Ye shall watch while nations strive
With the bloodhounds, die or survive,
Drop faint from their jaws,
Or throttle them backward to death;
And only under your breath
Shall favour the cause.
This is the curse. Write.

Ye shall watch while strong men draw
The nets of feudal law
To strangle the weak;
And, counting the sin for a sin,
Your soul shall be sadder within
Than the word ye shall speak.
This is the curse. Write.

When good men are praying erect
That Christ may avenge His elect
And deliver the earth,
The prayer in your ears, said low,
Shall sound like the tramp of a foe
That's driving you forth.
This is the curse. Write.

When wise men give you their praise,
They shall pause in the heat of the phrase,
As if carried too far.
When ye boast your own charters kept true,
Ye shall blush; for the thing which ye do

Derides what ye are.
This is the curse. Write.

When fools cast taunts at your gate,
Your scorn ye shall somewhat abate
As ye look o'er the wall;
For your conscience, tradition, and name
Explode with a deadlier blame
Than the worst of them all.
This is the curse. Write.

Go, wherever ill deeds shall be done,
Go, plant your flag in the sun
Beside the ill-doers!
And recoil from clenching the curse
Of God's witnessing Universe
With a curse of yours.
THIS is the curse. Write.

Nature's Remorses

Her soul was bred by a throne, and fed
  From the sucking-bottle used in her race
    On starch and water (for mother's milk
Which gives a larger growth instead),
  And, out of the natural liberal grace,
    Was swaddled away in violet silk.

And young and kind, and royally blind,
  Forth she stepped from her palace-door
    On three-piled carpet of compliments,
Curtains of incense drawn by the wind
  In between her for evermore
    And daylight issues of events.

On she drew, as a queen might do,
  To meet a Dream of Italy, –
    Of magical town and musical wave,
Where even a god, his amulet blue
  Of shining sea, in an ecstasy
    Dropt and forgot in a Nereid's cave.

Down she goes, as the soft wind blows,
  To live more smoothly than mortals can,
    To love and to reign as queen and wife,
To wear a crown that smells of a rose,
  And still, with a sceptre as light as a fan,
    Beat sweet time to the song of life.

What is this? As quick as a kiss
  Falls the smile from her girlish mouth!

The lion-people has left its lair,
Roaring along her garden of bliss,
  And the fiery underworld of the South
    Scorched a way to the upper air.

And a fire-stone ran in the form of a man,
  Burningly, boundingly, fatal and fell,
    Bowling the kingdom down! Where was the King?
She had heard somewhat, since life began,
  Of terrors on earth and horrors in hell,
    But never, never of such a thing.

You think she dropped when her dream was stopped,
  When the blotch of Bourbon blood inlay,
    Lividly rank, her new lord's cheek?
Not so. Her high heart overtopped
  The royal part she had come to play.
    Only the men in that hour were weak.

And twice a wife by her ravaged life,
  And twice a queen by her kingdom lost,
    She braved the shock and the counter-shock
Of hero and traitor, bullet and knife,
  While Italy pushed, like a vengeful ghost,
    That son of the Cursed from Gaeta's rock.

What will ye give her, who could not deliver,
  German Princesses? A laurel-wreath
    All over-scored with your signatures,
Graces, Serenities, Highnesses ever?
  Mock her not, fresh from the truth of Death,
    Conscious of dignities higher than yours.

What will ye put in your casket shut,
   Ladies of Paris, in sympathy's name?
     Guizot's daughter, what have you brought her?
Withered immortelles, long ago cut
   For guilty dynasties perished in shame,
     Putrid to memory, Guizot's daughter?

Ah poor queen! so young and serene!
   What shall we do for her, now hope's done,
     Standing at Rome in these ruins old,
She too a ruin and no more a queen?
   Leave her that diadem made by the sun
     Turning her hair to an innocent gold.

Ay! bring close to her, as 'twere a rose, to her,
   Yon free child from an Apennine city
     Singing for Italy, – dumb in the place!
Something like solace, let us suppose, to her
   Given, in that homage of wonder and pity,
     By his pure eyes to her beautiful face.

Nature, excluded, savagely brooded;
   Ruined all queendom and dogmas of state:
     Then, in reaction remorseful and mild,
Rescues the womanhood, nearly eluded,
   Shows her what's sweetest in womanly fate –
     Sunshine from Heaven, and the eyes of a child.

Lord Walter's Wife

'But why do you go?' said the lady, while both sat under
  the yew,
And her eyes were alive in their depth, as the kraken
  beneath the sea-blue.

'Because I fear you,' he answered; – 'because you are far
  too fair,
And able to strangle my soul in a mesh of your gold-
  coloured hair.'

'Oh, that,' she said, 'is no reason! Such knots are quickly
  undone,
And too much beauty, I reckon, is nothing but too much
  sun.'

'Yet farewell so,' he answered; – 'the sunstroke's fatal at
  times.
I value your husband, Lord Walter, whose gallop rings still
  from the limes.'

'Oh, that,' she said, 'is no reason. You smell a rose
  through a fence:
If two should smell it, what matter? who grumbles, and
  where's the pretence?'

'But I,' he replied, 'have promised another, when love was
  free,
To love her alone, alone, who alone and afar loves me.'

'Why, that,' she said, 'is no reason. Love's always free, I
   am told.
Will you vow to be safe from the headache on Tuesday,
   and think it will hold?'

'But you,' he replied, 'have a daughter, a young little
   child, who was laid
In your lap to be pure; so I leave you: the angels would
   make me afraid.'

'Oh, that,' she said, 'is no reason. The angels keep out of
   the way;
And Dora, the child, observes nothing, although you
   should please me and stay.'

At which he rose up in his anger, – 'Why, now, you no
   longer are fair!
Why, now, you no longer are fatal, but ugly and hateful, I
   swear.'

At which she laughed out in her scorn, – 'These men! O,
   these men overnice,
Who are shocked if a colour not virtuous is frankly put
   on by a vice.'

Her eyes blazed upon him – 'And you! You bring us your
   vices so near
That we smell them! you think in our presence a thought
   'twould defame us to hear!

'What reason had you, and what right, – I appeal to your
   soul from my life, –

To find me too fair as a woman? Why, sir, I am pure, and
a wife.

'Is the day-star too fair up above you? It burns you not.
Dare you imply
I brushed you more close than the star does, when Walter
had set me as high?

'If a man finds a woman too fair, he means simply
adapted too much
To uses unlawful and fatal. The praise! — shall I thank you
for such?

'Too fair? — not unless you misuse us! and surely if, once
in a while,
You attain to it, straightway you call us no longer too fair,
but too vile.

'A moment, — I pray your attention! — I have a poor word
in my head
I must utter, though womanly custom would set it down
better unsaid.

'You grew, sir, pale to impertinence, once when I showed
you a ring.
You kissed my fan when I dropped it. No matter! I've
broken the thing.

'You did me the honour, perhaps, to be moved at my side
now and then
In the senses, — a vice, I have heard, which is common to
beasts and some men.

'Love's a virtue for heroes! – as white as the snow on
    high hills,
And immortal as every great soul is that struggles,
    endures, and fulfils.

'I love my Walter profoundly, – you, Maude, though you
    faltered a week,
For the sake of ... what was it? an eyebrow? or, less still,
    a mole on a cheek?

'And since, when all's said, you're too noble to stoop to
    the frivolous cant
About crimes irresistible, virtues that swindle, betray and
    supplant,

'I determined to prove to yourself that, whate'er you
    might dream or avow
By illusion, you wanted precisely no more of me than
    you have now.

'There! Look me full in the face! – in the face.
    Understand, if you can,
That the eyes of such women as I am are clean as the
    palm of a man.

'Drop his hand, you insult him. Avoid us for fear we
    should cost you a scar, –
You take us for harlots, I tell you, and not for the women
    we are.

'You wronged me: but then I considered ... there's
    Walter! And so at the end,

I vowed that he should not be mulcted, by me, in the
   hand of a friend.

'Have I hurt you indeed? We are quits then. Nay, friend of
   my Walter, be mine!
Come, Dora, my darling, my angel, and help me to ask
   him to dine.'

Bianca Among the Nightingales

The cypress stood up like a church
   That night we felt our love would hold,
And saintly moonlight seemed to search
   And wash the whole world clean as gold;
The olives crystallised the vales'
   Broad slopes until the hills grew strong:
The fire-flies and the nightingales
   Throbbed each to either, flame and song.
The nightingales, the nightingales!

Upon the angle of its shade
   The cypress stood, self-balanced high;
Half up, half down, as double-made,
   Along the ground, against the sky;
And we, too! from such soul-height went
   Such leaps of blood, so blindly driven,
We scarce knew if our nature meant
   Most passionate earth or intense heaven
The nightingales, the nightingales!

We paled with love, we shook with love,
   We kissed so close we could not vow;
Till Giulio whispered 'Sweet, above
   God's Ever guaranties this Now.'
And through his words the nightingales
   Drove straight and full their long clear call,
Like arrows through heroic mails,
   And love was awful in it all.
The nightingales, the nightingales!

O cold white moonlight of the north,
  Refresh these pulses, quench this hell!
O coverture of death drawn forth
  Across this garden-chamber ... well!
But what have nightingales to do
  In gloomy England, called the free ...
(Yes, free to die in!...) when we two
  Are sundered, singing still to me?
And still they sing, the nightingales!

I think I hear him, how he cried
  'My own soul's life!' between their notes.
Each man has but one soul supplied,
  And that's immortal. Though his throat's
On fire with passion now, to her
  He can't say what to me he said!
And yet he moves her, they aver.
  The nightingales sing through my head, –
The nightingales, the nightingales!

He says to her what moves her most.
  He would not name his soul within
Her hearing, – rather pays her cost
  With praises to her lips and chin.
Man has but one soul, 'tis ordained,
  And each soul but one love, I add;
Yet souls are damned and love's profaned;
  These nightingales will sing me mad!
The nightingales, the nightingales!

I marvel how the birds can sing.
  There's little difference, in their view,

Betwixt our Tuscan trees that spring
  As vital flames into the blue,
And dull round blots of foliage meant,
  Like saturated sponges here,
To suck the fogs up. As content
  Is he too in this land, 'tis clear.
And still they sing, the nightingales.

My native Florence! dear, forgone!
  I see across the Alpine ridge
How the last feast-day of Saint John
  Shot rockets from Carraia bridge.
The luminous city, tall with fire,
  Trod deep down in that river of ours,
While many a boat with lamp and choir
  Skimmed birdlike over glittering towers.
I will not hear these nightingales.

I seem to float, *we* seem to float
  Down Arno's stream in festive guise;
A boat strikes flame into our boat,
  And up that lady seems to rise
As then she rose. The shock had flashed
  A vision on us! What a head,
What leaping eyeballs! – beauty dashed
  To splendour by a sudden dread.
And still they sing, the nightingales.

Too bold to sin, too weak to die;
  Such women are so. As for me,
I would we had drowned there, he and I,
  That moment, loving perfectly.

He had not caught her with her loosed
  Gold ringlets ... rarer in the south ...
Nor heard the '*Grazie tanto*' bruised
  To sweetness by her English mouth.
And still they sing, the nightingales.

She had not reached him at my heart
  With her fine tongue, as snakes indeed
Kill flies; nor had I, for my part,
  Yearned after, in my desperate need,
And followed him as he did her
  To coasts left bitter by the tide,
Whose very nightingales, elsewhere
  Delighting, torture and deride!
For still they sing, the nightingales.

A worthless woman; mere cold clay
  As all false things are: but so fair,
She takes the breath of men away
  Who gaze upon her unaware.
I would not play her larcenous tricks
  To have her looks! She lied and stole,
And spat into my love's pure pyx
  The rank saliva of her soul.
And still they sing, the nightingales.

I would not for her white and pink,
  Though such he likes − her grace of limb,
Though such he has praised − nor yet, I think.
  For life itself, though spent with him,
Commit such sacrilege, affront
  God's nature which is love, intrude

'Twixt two affianced souls, and hunt
  Like spiders, in the altar's wood.
I cannot bear these nightingales.

If she chose sin, some gentler guise
  She might have sinned in, so it seems:
She might have pricked out both my eyes,
  And I still seen him in my dreams!
– Or drugged me in my soup or wine,
  Nor left me angry afterward:
To die here with his hand in mine,
  His breath upon me, were not hard.
(Our Lady hush these nightingales!)

But set a springe for him, 'mio ben,'
  My only good, my first last love! –
Though Christ knows well what sin is, when
  He sees some things done they must move
Himself to wonder. Let her pass.
  I think of her by night and day.
Must I too join her ... out, alas!...
  With Giulio, in each word I say?
And evermore the nightingales!

Giulio, my Giulio! – sing they so,
  And you be silent? Do I speak,
And you not hear? An arm you throw
  Round someone, and I feel so weak?
– Oh, owl-like birds! They sing for spite,
  They sing for hate, they sing for doom,
They'll sing through death who sing through night,
  They'll sing and stun me in the tomb –
The nightingales, the nightingales!

My Heart and I

Enough! we're tired, my heart and I.
　We sit beside the headstone thus,
　And wish that name were carv'd for us.
The moss reprints more tenderly
　The hard types of the mason's knife,
　As heaven's sweet life renews earth's life
With which we're tired, my heart and I.

You see we're tired, my heart and I.
　We dealt with books, we trusted men,
　And in our own blood drench'd the pen,
As if such colours could not fly.
　We walk'd too straight for fortune's end,
　We lov'd too true to keep a friend;
At last we're tired, my heart and I.

How tired we feel, my heart and I!
　We seem of no use in the world;
　Our fancies hang grey and uncurl'd
About men's eyes indifferently;
　Our voice which thrill'd you so, will let
　You sleep; our tears are only wet:
What do we here, my heart and I?

So tired, so tired, my heart and I!
　It was not thus in that old time
　When Ralph sat with me 'neath the lime
To watch the sunset from the sky.
　'Dear love, you're looking tired,' he said;

I, smiling at him, shook my head.
'Tis now we're tired, my heart and I.

So tired, so tired, my heart and I!
  Though now none takes me on his arm
  To fold me close and kiss me warm
Till each quick breath end in a sigh
  Of happy languor. Now, alone,
  We lean upon this graveyard stone,
Uncheer'd, unkiss'd, my heart and I.

Tired out we are, my heart and I.
  Suppose the world brought diadems
  To tempt us, crusted with loose gems
Of powers and pleasures? Let it try.
  We scarcely care to look at even
  A pretty child, or God's blue heaven,
We feel so tired, my heart and I.

Yet who complains? My heart and I?
  In this abundant earth no doubt
  Is little room for things worn out:
Disdain them, break them, throw them by!
  And if before the days grew rough
  We *once* were lov'd, us'd, – well enough,
I think, we've far'd, my heart and I.

Mother and Poet

Dead! One of them shot by the sea in the east,
  And one of them shot in the west by the sea.
Dead! both my boys! When you sit at the feast
  And are wanting a great song for Italy free,
    Let none look at me!

Yet I was a poetess only last year,
  And good at my art, for a woman, men said;
But this woman, this, who is agonised here,
  — The east sea and west sea rhyme on in her head
    For ever instead.

What art can a woman be good at? Oh, vain!
  What art is she good at, but hurting her breast
With the milk-teeth of babes, and a smile at the pain?
  Ah, boys, how you hurt! you were strong as you
    pressed,
    And I proud, by that test.

What art's for a woman? To hold on her knees
  Both darlings! to feel all their arms round her throat,
Cling, strangle a little! to sew by degrees
  And 'broider the long-clothes and neat little coat;
    To dream and to dote.

To teach them ... It stings there! I made them indeed
  Speak plain the word country. I taught them, no doubt,
That a country's a thing men should die for at need.
  I prated of liberty, rights, and about
    The tyrant cast out.

And when their eyes flashed ... O my beautiful eyes! ...
  I exulted; nay, let them go forth at the wheels
Of the guns, and denied not. But then the surprise
  When one sits quite alone! Then one weeps, then one
    kneels!
    God, how the house feels!

At first, happy news came, in gay letters moiled
  With my kisses, – of camp-life and glory, and how
They both loved me; and, soon coming home to be
  spoiled,
  In return would fan off every fly from my brow
    With their green laurel-bough.

Then was triumph at Turin: Ancona was free!
  And some one came out of the cheers in the street,
With a face pale as stone, to say something to me.
  My Guido was dead! I fell down at his feet,
    While they cheered in the street.

I bore it; friends soothed me; my grief looked sublime
  As the ransom of Italy. One boy remained
To be leant on and walked with, recalling the time
  When the first grew immortal, while both of us
    strained
    To the height he had gained.

And letters still came, shorter, sadder, more strong,
  Writ now but in one hand, 'I was not to faint, –
One loved me for two – would be with me ere long:
  And *Viva l' Italia!* – he died for, our saint,
    Who forbids our complaint.'

My Nanni would add, 'he was safe, and aware
  Of a presence that turned off the balls, – was imprest
It was Guido himself, who knew what I could bear,
  And how 'twas impossible, quite dispossessed,
    To live on for the rest.'

On which, without pause, up the telegraph line
  Swept smoothly the next news from Gaeta: – Shot.
Tell his mother. Ah, ah, 'his', 'their' mother, – not 'mine',
  No voice says 'My mother' again to me. What!
    You think Guido forgot?

Are souls straight so happy that, dizzy with Heaven,
  They drop earth's affections, conceive not of woe?
I think not. Themselves were too lately forgiven
  Through THAT Love and Sorrow which reconciled so
    The Above and Below.

O Christ of the five wounds, who look'dst through the
  dark
  To the face of Thy mother! consider, I pray,
How we common mothers stand desolate, mark,
  Whose sons, not being Christs, die with eyes turned
    away,
    And no last word to say!

Both boys dead? but that's out of nature. We all
  Have been patriots, yet each house must always
    keep one.
'Twere imbecile, hewing out roads to a wall;
  And, when Italy's made, for what end is it done
    If we have not a son?

Ah, ah, ah! when Gaeta's taken, what then?
  When the fair wicked queen sits no more at her sport
Of the fire-balls of death crashing souls out of men?
  When the guns of Cavalli with final retort
    Have cut the game short?

When Venice and Rome keep their new jubilee,
  When your flag takes all heaven for its white, green,
    and red,
When you have your country from mountain to sea,
  When King Victor has Italy's crown on his head,
    (And I have my Dead) —

What then? Do not mock me. Ah, ring your bells low,
  And burn your lights faintly! My country is there,
Above the star pricked by the last peak of snow:
  My Italy's THERE, with my brave civic Pair,
    To disfranchise despair!

Forgive me. Some women bear children in strength,
  And bite back the cry of their pain in self-scorn;
But the birth-pangs of nations will wring us at length
  Into wail such as this — and we sit on forlorn
    When the man-child is born.

Dead! One of them shot by the sea in the east,
  And one of them shot in the west by the sea.
Both! both my boys! If in keeping the feast
  You want a great song for your Italy free,
    Let none look at me!

De Profundis

The Face which, duly as the sun,
Rose up for me with life begun,
To mark all bright hours of the day
With daily love, is dimmed away, –
And yet my days go on, go on.

The tongue which, like a stream, could run
Smooth music from the roughest stone,
And every morning with 'Good day'
Make each day good, is hushed away, –
And yet my days go on, go on.

The heart which, like a staff, was one
For mine to lean and rest upon,
The strongest on the longest day
With steadfast love, is caught away, –
And yet my days go on, go on.

And cold before my summer's clone,
And deaf in Nature's general tune,
And fallen too low for special fear,
And here, with hope no longer here, –
While the tears drop, my days go on.

The world goes whispering to its own,
'This anguish pierces to the bone';
And tender friends go sighing round,
'What love can ever cure this wound?'
My days go on, my days go on.

The past rolls forward on the sun
And makes all night. O dreams begun,
Not to be ended! Ended bliss,
And life that will not end in this!
My days go on, my days go on.

Breath freezes on my lips to moan:
As one alone, once not alone,
I sit and knock at Nature's door,
Heart-bare, heart-hungry, very poor,
Whose desolated days go on.

I knock and cry, – Undone, undone!
Is there no help, no comfort, – none?
No gleaning in the wide wheat-plains
Where others drive their loaded wains?
My vacant days go on, go on.

This Nature, though the snows be down,
Thinks kindly of the bird of June:
The little red hip on the tree
Is ripe for such. What is for me,
Whose days so winterly go on?

No bird am I to sing in June,
And dare not ask an equal boon.
Good nests and berries red are Nature's
To give away to better creatures, –
And yet my days go on, go on.

I ask less kindness to be done, –
Only to loose these pilgrim-shoon

(Too early worn and grimed), with sweet
Cool deathly touch to these tired feet,
Till days go out which now go on.

Only to lift the turf unmown
From off the earth where it has grown,
Some cubit-space, and say, 'Behold,
Creep in, poor Heart, beneath that fold,
Forgetting how the days go on.'

What harm would that do? Green anon
The sword would quicken, overshone
By skies as blue; as crickets might
Have leave to chirp there day and night
While my new rest went on, went on.

From gracious Nature have I won
Such liberal bounty? may I run
So, lizard-like, within her side,
And there be safe, who now am tried
By days that painfully go on?

– A Voice reproves me thereupon,
More sweet than Nature's, when the drone
Of bees is sweetest, and more deep
Than when the rivers overleap
The shuddering pines, and thunder on.

God's Voice, not Nature's! Night and noon
He sits upon the great white throne,
And listens for the creature's praise.

What babble we of days and days?
The Dayspring He, whose days go on!

He reigns above, He reigns alone;
Systems burn out and leave His throne;
Fair mists of seraphs melt and fall
Around Him, changeless amid all, –
Ancient of Days, whose days go on.

He reigns below, He reigns alone,
And, having life in love forgone
Beneath the crown of sovran thorns,
He reigns the jealous God. Who mourns
Or rules with Him, while days go on?

By anguish which made pale the sun,
I hear Him charge His saints that none
Among His creatures anywhere
Blaspheme against Him with despair,
However darkly days go on.

Take from my head the thorn-wreath brown!
No mortal grief deserves that crown.
O súpreme Love, chief Misery,
The sharp regalia are for THEE,
Whose days eternally go on!

For us, – whatever's undergone,
Thou knowest, willest what is done.
Grief may be joy misunderstood;
Only the Good discerns the good.
I trust Thee while my days go on.

Whatever's lost, it first was won:
We will not struggle nor impugn.
Perhaps the cup was broken here,
That Heaven's new wine might show more clear.
I praise Thee while my days go on.

I praise Thee while my days go on;
I love Thee while my days go on:
Through dark and dearth, through fire and frost,
With emptied arms and treasure lost,
I thank Thee while my days go on!

And having in Thy life-depth thrown
Being and suffering (which are one),
As a child drops some pebble small
Down some deep well, and hears it fall
Smiling — so I. THY DAYS GO ON.

Died ...

What shall we add now? He is dead.
And I who praise and you who blame,
With wash of words across his name,
Find suddenly declared instead –
'On Sunday, third of August, dead.'

Which stops the whole we talked to-day.
I quickened to a plausive glance
At his large general tolerance
By common people's narrow way,
Stopped short in praising. Dead, they say.

And you, who had just put in a sort
Of cold deduction – 'rather, large
Through weakness of the continent marge,
Than greatness of the thing contained' –
Broke off. Dead! – there, you stood restrained.

As if we had talked in following one
Up some long gallery. 'Would you choose
An air like that? The gait is loose –
Or noble.' Sudden in the sun
An oubliette winks. Where is he? Gone.

Dead. Man's 'I was' by God's 'I am' –
All hero-worship comes to that.
High heart, high thought, high fame, as flat
As a gravestone. Bring your Jacet jam –
The epitaph's an epigram.

Dead. There's an answer to arrest
All carping. Dust's his natural place?
He'll let the flies buzz round his face
And, though you slander, not protest?
– From such an one, exact the Best?

Opinions gold or brass are null.
We chuck our flattery or abuse,
Called Caesar's due, as Charon's dues,
I' the teeth of some dead sage or fool,
To mend the grinning of a skull.

Be abstinent in praise and blame.
The man's still mortal, who stands first,
And mortal only, if last and worst.
Then slowly lift so frail a fame,
Or softly drop so poor a shame.

A Musical Instrument

What was he doing, the great god Pan,
  Down in the reeds by the river?
Spreading ruin and scattering ban,
Splashing and paddling with hoofs of a goat,
And breaking the golden lilies afloat
  With the dragon-fly on the river.

He tore out a reed, the great god Pan,
  From the deep cool bed of the river:
The limpid water turbidly ran,
And the broken lilies a-dying lay,
And the dragon-fly had fled away,
  Ere he brought it out of the river.

High on the shore sat the great god Pan,
  While turbidly flowed the river;
And hacked and hewed as a great god can,
With his hard bleak steel at the patient reed,
Till there was not a sign of a leaf indeed
  To prove it fresh from the river.

He cut it short, did the great god Pan,
  (How tall it stood in the river!)
Then drew the pith, like the heart of a man,
Steadily from the outside ring,
And notch'd the poor dry empty thing
  In holes, as he sat by the river.

'This is the way,' laughed the great god Pan,
  (Laughed while he sat by the river),

'The only way, since gods began
To make sweet music, they could succeed.'
Then, dropping his mouth to a hole in the reed,
    He blew in power by the river.

Sweet, sweet, sweet, O Pan!
    Piercing sweet by the river!
Blinding sweet, O great god Pan!
The sun on the hill forgot to die,
And the lilies revived, and the dragon-fly
    Came back to dream on the river.

Yet half a beast is the great god Pan,
    To laugh as he sits by the river,
Making a poet out of a man:
The true gods sigh for the cost and pain,
For the reed which grows nevermore again
    As a reed with the reeds in the river.

Index